FAITH FUSION
Elementary Edition

Knowing, Loving, and Serving Christ in the Catholic Church

Gloria Shahin

Foreword
Rev. Alfred McBride, O.Praem.

Our Sunday Visitor

osv.com
faithfusion.com

Our Sunday Visitor Publishing Division
Our Sunday Visitor, Inc.
Huntington, Indiana 46750

Credits

Reviewers/Consultants: Heidi Busse; Margaret DeMatteo; Rev. Alfred McBride, O.Praem.; Rita Burns-Senseman

General Editor: David Dziena

Cover and Interior Design, Photo Research: Lindsey Riesen

Cover Image: Artwork is by Jen Norton. Find more information about this artist and purchase art prints at www.JenNortonArtStudio.com

Nihil Obstat
Msgr. Michael Heintz, Ph.D.
Censor Librorum

Imprimatur
✠ Kevin C. Rhoades
Bishop of Fort Wayne-South Bend

The *Nihil Obstat* and *Imprimatur* are official declarations that a book or pamphlet is free of doctrinal and moral error. No implication is contained therein that those who have granted the *Nihil Obstat* and *Imprimatur* agree with the contents, opinions, or statements expressed.

For more information, visit www.osv.com/permissions

Our Sunday Visitor Publishing Division
Our Sunday Visitor, Inc.
200 Noll Plaza
Huntington, Indiana 46750
1-800-348-2440

Acknowledgments
Scripture selections taken from the *New American Bible, Revised Edition* © 2010, 1991, 1986, 1970 by the Confraternity of Christian Doctrine, Washington, D.C., and are used by license of the copyright owner. All rights reserved. No part of the *New American Bible* may be reproduced in any form without permission in writing from the copyright owner.

Excerpts from the English translation of the *Catechism of the Catholic Church* for use in the United States of America copyright © 1994, United States Catholic Conference, Inc.—Libreria Editrice Vaticana. English translation of the *Catechism of the Catholic Church*: Modifications from the Editio Typica copyright © 1997, United States Catholic Conference, Inc.—Libreria Editrice Vaticana. Used by permission. All rights reserved.

Excerpts from the English translation of *Rite of Baptism for Children* © 1969, International Commission on English in the Liturgy Corporation (ICEL); excerpts from the English translation of *Rite of Penance* © 1974, ICEL; excerpts from the English translation of *The Roman Missal* © 2010, ICEL. All rights reserved.

Printed in 2022
ISBN: 978-1-61278-737-4
Inventory No. X1447

Image Credits: **3** The Crosiers **4** The Crosiers, see pg 86 credit **5, 6, 8** Thinkstock **9, 10, 11** Shutterstock **13** Thinkstock **14** Our Sunday Visitor **16** CNS **18** The Crosiers, Shutterstock **19** Shutterstock, Thinkstock **21** Shutterstock **22** Our Sunday Visitor **23** Thinkstock **24** The Crosiers **26** Our Sunday Visitor, Shutterstock **27** Shutterstock **29** Standard Publishing/Licensed from GoodSalt.com **30** DeAgnostini Picture Library/Bridgeman Images **31** Our Sunday Visitor, Thinkstock **32** Our Sunday Visitor **34** Shutterstock, W.P. Wittman, Ltd. **35, 37, 38** Shutterstock **39, 40** Thinkstock **41** Our Sunday Vistior **42** The Crosiers, Shutterstock **43, 45** Shutterstock **46** Our Sunday Visitor **48** Shutterstock **49** Sam Lucero **50** The Crosiers, CNS **51** Our Sunday Visitor, Shutterstock **53** Shutterstock **54** Private Collection/Bridgeman Images **55, 56** Shutterstock **58** Artwork of Saint Dominic Savio is by Jen Norton. Find more information about this artist and purchase art prints at www.JenNortonArtStudio.com, The Crosiers **59** Thinkstock **61** Shutterstock **62** Jim West/Alamy **64, 65** Shutterstock **66** Artwork of Saint Dismas is by Jen Norton. Find more information about this artist and purchase art prints at www.JenNortonArtStudio.com **67, 69** Shutterstock **71** Jim Olvera **72** Shane Johnson **73** Sam Lucero **74** The Crosiers **75** W.P. Wittman, Ltd. **76** Our Sunday Vistior **78** Artwork of Saint Clare of Assisi is by Jen Norton. Find more information about this artist and purchase art prints at www.JenNortonArtStudio.com, EyePics **79** Shutterstock **81** Jim Olvera **82** Standard Publishing/Licensed from GoodSalt.com **83** Shutterstock **84** W.P. Wittman, Ltd. **85** Shane Johnson **86** Artwork of Saint John the Baptist is by Jen Norton. Find more information about this artist and purchase art prints at www.JenNortonArtStudio.com, Shutterstock **87** Shutterstock **89** Jim Olvera **90** Dioceasan Museum, Wloclawek, PolandAlinari/Bridgeman Images **91** Veer, Thinkstock **92** W.P. Wittman, Ltd. **93** Shutterstock **94** Agnus Images, EyePics **95** Our Sunday Visitor **97** Sam Lucero **98** Our Sunday Visitor, W.P. Wittman Ltd. **100** W.P. Wittman Ltd. **101** Shutterstock **102** Artwork of Saint Joseph is by Jen Norton. Find more information about this artist and purchase art prints at www.JenNortonArtStudio.com, Shutterstock **103** Shutterstock **107** Thinkstock **108** Shutterstock **109** Thinkstock **110** Providence Collection/Licensed from GoodSalt.com **111** Shutterstock **112** Private Collection The Stapleton Collection/Bridgeman Images **113** Thinkstock, Shutterstock **114** Our Sunday Visitor, Shutterstock **115** Thinkstock, Shutterstock **117** Shutterstock **118** Our Sunday Visitor, The Crosiers **119** Shutterstock **120** Thinkstock **121** Shutterstock **122** Artwork of Saint Michael the Archangel is by Jen Norton. Find more information about this artist and purchase art prints at www.JenNortonArtStudio.com, W.P. Wittman Ltd. **123, 125** Thinkstock **126** Our Sunday Vistior **128, 129** Shutterstock **130** The Crosiers, Shutterstock **131** Thinkstock **133** Shutterstock **134** Our Sunday Visitor, The Crosiers **135** Thinkstock, W.P. Wittman Ltd. **137** Shutterstock **138** Our Sunday Visitor, Shutterstock **136** Thinkstock **141** Shutterstock **142** Providence Collection/Licensed from GoodSalt.com **143, 144** Shutterstock **145** Our Sunday Vistior, Veer **146** Newscom **147** Veer **149** Thinkstock **150** Providence Collection/Licensed from GoodSalt.com **151** Shutterstock **153** Our Sunday Visitor **154** The Crosiers, Shutterstock **155** Thinkstock **157, 159, 160, 161** Shutterstock **162** Providence Collection/Licensed from GoodSalt.com **164** Thinkstock **165** Standard Publishing/Licensed from GoodSalt.com **166** Our Sunday Visitor, Shutterstock **167** CNS **169** The Crosiers **170** Our Sunday Vistior, Providence Collection /Licensed from GoodSalt.com **171** Thinkstock **172** Jim Olvera **173** Thinkstock **174** Our Sunday Visitor, Shutterstock **175** Jim Olvera **177** Jim Olvera **178** Shutterstock **179** Thinkstock **180** Keith Dannemiller/Alamy **182** Shutterstock, Our Sunday Visitor **183** Thinkstock **186** Shutterstock **191** Thinkstock **192** Friedrich Stark/Almay, Thinkstock **193** Providence Collection /Licensed from GoodSalt.com **195** Shutterstock, Jim Olvera **196** Jim Olvera **197** Thinkstock **198** The Crosiers **199** The Annunciation/Henry Ossawa Tanner/Philadelphia Museum of Art **201** Shutterstock **202** The Crosiers **203** Thinkstock **205** ZUMA Press, Inc./Almay **208** CNS **209** DesignPics **211** W.P. Wittman Ltd. **213** The Crosiers **214** Thinkstock **216** Shutterstock **Poster: Side 1:** The Crosiers **Side 2:** The Crosiers, Shutterstock, Providence Collection/Licensed from GoodSalt.com, Providence Collection/Licensed from GoodSalt.com, Standard Publishing/Licensed from GoodSalt.com, Private Collection Ken Welsh/Bridgeman Images, Providence Collection/Licensed from GoodSalt.com, Musee Conde, Chantilly, France/Bridgeman Images, The Crosiers, W.P. Wittman, Ltd.

Sheridan, Madison, WI, USA; April 2022, Job# 2111258

Table of Contents

Unit 1: The Profession of Faith

Unit 2: The Celebration of the Christian Mystery

Unit 3: Life in Christ

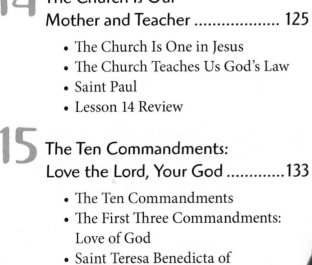

Unit 4: Christian Prayer

A two-sided pullout poster features:

- A Bible timeline covering key events of Salvation History, from Creation to Pentecost and the Early Church.

- Great People of the Bible includes key Old Testament and New Testament people, including Abraham, Noah, Mary, Jesus, and the Apostles. See page 192.

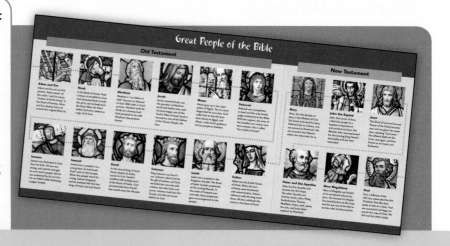

Foreword

In reading *Faith Fusion* I kept saying to myself, "Wholeness," a buzzword from psychology, but actually fulfilled in this user-friendly text. I commend the author for designing a tapestry in true renaissance style instead of a narrow teaching tool, seeming to have forgotten nothing in thinking of ways to make Catholic teaching accessible and a relationship with Christ credible.

Here you will find prayer, Sacred Scripture, Sacred Tradition, liturgy, saints' lives and Catholic customs and practices presented in an integrated manner.

Woven into these elements are recurrent forms of life applications: What does it mean to you? How does this make you a better Catholic? How does this help you to want the best for yourselves and others? Readers will have little chance to idly wonder over this or that aspect of a teaching.

Every lesson contains a story of a saint, a practice that dates in catechesis from the earliest days of the Church. The power of a personal witness story inspires and motivates the listener to act on the teaching that is illustrated—and is effectively used in this text.

Everyone profits from a "catch-up" from time to time. This is especially true when one is in transition, such as during preparation for the Sacraments of Eucharist or Confirmation, participation in RCIA, and when entering faith formation for the first time (or re-entering) in later grades.

Clear, direct, and challenging, this text owns a simplicity that is admirable. Distilled wisdom always is.

The author wisely followed the sequence of the four pillars of the *Catechism of the Catholic Church*: Creed, Liturgy, Life in Christ, Prayer. These pillars lead the learner to ponder the faith believed, the faith celebrated, the faith in moral practice, and the faith prayed.

This approach invites children to hear the voice of the Father and see the face of Christ and live in the house of the Church with the Holy Spirit. It gives them a map of life for this earth and the goal of eternal life hereafter.

Rev. Alfred McBride, O.Praem

Prayer of Discipleship

Loving God,
I thank you for choosing me
to be your disciple
and for the gift of your Son, Jesus.
Help me proclaim and bear witness
to the Gospel
by word and by deed
today and every day.
Open my heart to the outcast,
the forgotten, the lonely,
the sick, and the poor.
Grant me the courage to think,
choose, and live as a Christian,
joyfully obedient to God.
Amen.

*Adapted from the Homily of
Pope Francis, Basilica of Saint Paul
Outside-the-Walls, Third Sunday of
Easter, April 14, 2013*

BEING CATHOLIC

God Loves Us and Calls Us by Name

God is our heavenly Father. He created us out of love. Even before we were born, God loved us and wanted us to belong to him. We are very special to God. He loves us with no strings attached. And he will love us forever no matter what. In the Bible we read:

> Before birth the LORD called me,
> from my mother's womb he gave me my name.
> —Isaiah 49:1

These words from the Book of Isaiah tell us that God knew us and loved us before we were born. They tell us that God created us for himself, to live in happiness with him.

What Is Love?

Love means _____

_____

These are ways I show love for …

my family:_____

my friends: _____

God's creation: _____

These are ways God shows love "with no strings attached" for me:

_____

_____

_____

God Gave Me a Special Identity

God created each of us with a unique identity. Each of us has a special place in God's plan for the world. You have a special place in your family, among your friends, and in every group you belong to. Your identity begins with your name. But it is so much more than that. It is also all the special qualities and talents that make you *you*.

Through the special gifts and talents God gave you, you can share special relationships with other people. Through your words you can show love and kindness to others, and help others in many ways. Through your actions you can bring joy to other people. You can also use your gifts and talents to grow closer to God. You can talk to God in prayer, you can praise him in song, you can glorify him through art. You can also grow closer to God when you do good things for others.

Who Am I?

Complete these sentences to tell some things about yourself, then in the mirror, draw a picture of yourself.

My name is _____

My name means _____

I was given this name because _____

_____

My special talents are _____

_____

My favorite way to put these talents to use is _____

_____

_____

The Profession of Faith

The one true God, our Creator and Lord, can be known with certainty from his works, by the natural light of human reason. (*CCC*, 47)

The Nicene Creed

I believe in one God,
the Father almighty,
maker of heaven and earth,
of all things visible and invisible.
I believe in one Lord Jesus Christ,
the Only Begotten Son of God,
born of the Father before all ages.
God from God, Light from Light,
true God from true God,
begotten, not made,
consubstantial with the Father;
through him all things were made.
For us men and for our salvation
he came down from heaven,
and by the Holy Spirit was incarnate
of the Virgin Mary,
and became man.
For our sake he was crucified
under Pontius Pilate,
he suffered death and was buried,
and rose again on the third day
in accordance with the Scriptures.
He ascended into heaven
and is seated at the right hand of the Father.
He will come again in glory
to judge the living and the dead
and his kingdom will have no end.
I believe in the Holy Spirit, the Lord,
the giver of life,
who proceeds from the Father and the Son,
who with the Father and the Son
is adored and glorified,
who has spoken through the prophets.
I believe in one, holy,
catholic and apostolic Church.
I confess one baptism for the forgiveness of sins
and I look forward to
the resurrection of the dead
and the life of the world to come.
Amen.

God Calls Us to Know Him and Love Him

Let Us Pray

A Psalm Prayer

Your word, LORD, stands forever;
    it is firm as the heavens.
Through all generations your truth endures;
    fixed to stand firm like the earth.
Your word is a lamp for my feet,
    a light for my path.
Your testimonies are my heritage forever;
    they are the joy of my heart.

—Psalm 119:89–90, 105, 111

My Catholic Faith

We can learn about God and how he wants us to live by reading the Bible.

➡ **How often do you read or hear God's Word in the Bible?**

Sacred Scripture

Do you know the two main parts of the Bible? They are the Old Testament and the New Testament. The Scripture passage you are about to read comes from the New Testament, from a book called the Letter to the Hebrews. The Hebrews were a community of early Christians. In this passage, we hear how important it is to have **faith** in God. We are told that without faith we cannot know God or love him.

Faith Leads Us to God

Faith is believing in what we cannot see. Through faith we believe that God created the universe. We also believe that what we see in the universe is because of God's goodness.

It is impossible to please God without faith. If we call on God, we must believe that he exists. We must believe that he rewards those who want to know him.

Noah, Abraham, and Moses had great faith in God. Because of their faith, God did wonderful things for Israel.

By faith in God's word, Noah built an ark for the salvation of his household.

By faith, Abraham went to a strange land, and he and Sarah had many descendants.

By faith, Moses led the Israelites across the Red Sea.

We are surrounded by many witnesses. Let us rid ourselves of the burden of sin, and keep our eyes fixed on Jesus, whose faith was perfect.

—Based on Hebrews 11:1–29, 12:1–2

Scripture at Mass

We hear Sacred Scripture proclaimed at Mass. This part of Mass is called the Liturgy of the Word. In the Liturgy of the Word we usually hear three Scripture readings and pray one Psalm. The Scripture passage from Hebrews that you just read would be the Second Reading.

Living the Scripture

In the Scripture passage from the Letter to the Hebrews we get to know holy people who lived a long time ago. These people had great faith in God.

Who do you know who shows great faith in God? In the space below, tell about this person and how his or her example helps you grow in faith. Add a picture to your response. The picture can be of the person or something that represents the person.

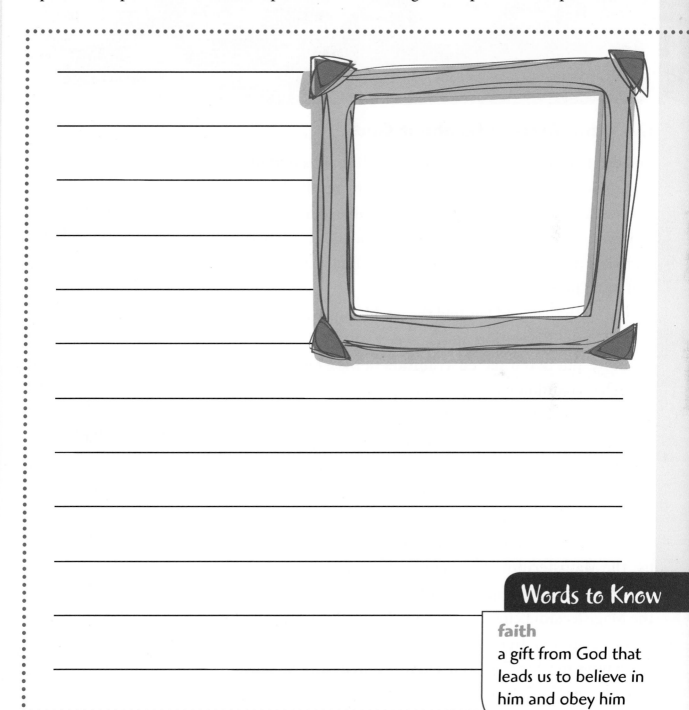

Words to Know

faith
a gift from God that leads us to believe in him and obey him

Our Catholic Tradition

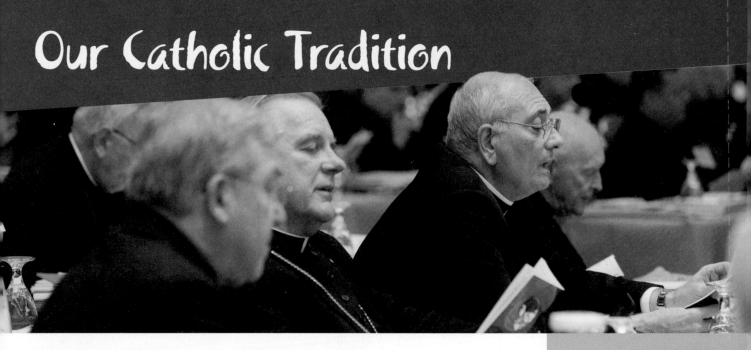

The Bible Teaches Us about God

God created us to live in happiness with him. It is part of human nature to want to know God and to be with him. God will always be a mystery we are not able to understand. However, reading **Sacred Scripture**, or the Bible, will help us get to know him and love him more. The Bible is God's Word written in human words.

The truth that God has told the world about himself is called **Divine Revelation**. Revelation is found in Sacred Scripture and in the **Sacred Tradition** of the Church. The Church's Tradition includes everything Jesus taught and that the Apostles passed on. Tradition is made up of the Church's teachings, life, and worship. With the guidance of the Holy Spirit, the Church helps us understand God's Divine Revelation and what it means for our lives. The Church passes on this understanding to all people, in all times and places.

It is important for all people to understand what God tells us. The **Magisterium**, the teaching office of the Church, helps us with this understanding. With the help of the Holy Spirit, the Magisterium helps us understand Sacred Scripture and Sacred Tradition. In interpreting Scripture, the Magisterium is attentive to what God wants to reveal to us for our salvation. Listening to God's Word and following the Church's teaching keeps us on the path to God.

Whose words are in the Bible?

Who helps us understand what God tells us in the Bible?

What is the Magisterium?

Live Your Faith

Complete the crossword puzzle using the following clues.

Across

1. _____ is a gift from God that leads us to believe in him and obey him.

5. The truth that God has told the world about himself is called _____ Revelation.

7. Our faith in _____ leads us to turn to him as our Creator.

Down

2. God created us to live in _____ with him.

3. The _____ is another name for Sacred Scripture.

4. Listening to the Bible and following the Church's _____ keeps us on the path to God.

6. The Bible is God's _____ written by human hands.

Words to Know

Sacred Scripture another name for the Bible; Sacred Scripture is the Word of God written by humans

Divine Revelation the way God makes himself, and his plan for all people, known to us

Sacred Tradition God's Word handed down to all the faithful in the Church's creeds, Sacraments, and other teachings

Magisterium the teaching office of the Church, which is all of the bishops in union with the Pope

Saints and Holy People

Saint Matthew the Evangelist (first century AD)

Remember that there are two main parts in the Bible: the Old Testament and the New Testament. The New Testament begins with the four Gospels. Saint Matthew is the writer of one of the Gospels.

Saint Matthew was one of Jesus' twelve Apostles. Matthew was a Jew, but other Jews did not like him. This was because Matthew's job was to collect taxes for the Roman government. They were surprised when Jesus asked Matthew to be one of his disciples.

Saint Matthew finished writing his Gospel around AD 85. This was about fifty years after Jesus' death. He began the Gospel with a genealogy, or family history, of Jesus. He did this to connect Jesus to Old Testament fathers of faith, such as Abraham and King David. This also showed that God's work in the Old Testament continued in Jesus Christ. People who read Matthew's Gospel understood that Jesus was a teacher and Savior for all.

Matthew's Gospel and the other Gospels help us know about Jesus. They tell us about Jesus' life on earth and of his great love for all people. The Church celebrates Saint Matthew's feast day on September 21.

Catholic Customs   Symbols for the Gospel Writers

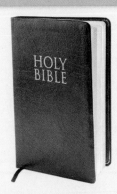

The Gospels have the most important place in the Bible because they tell us about Jesus. The writers of the four Gospels are called the evangelists. They are Matthew, Mark, Luke, and John.

In Church art, symbols are sometimes used for the evangelists. You can see the symbol for Matthew and the other Gospel writers above. Matthew's symbol is an angel. The symbols for the other evangelists are a winged ox for Luke, a winged lion for Mark, and an eagle for John.

Make It Happen

Saint Matthew wrote about Jesus to help people believe in him. Now it is your turn to teach others about Jesus. In the space below, tell three things you know about Jesus that can help your family or friends know and believe in him.

1. _____

2. _____

3. _____

Faith at Home

Saint Matthew's Gospel teaches about Jesus' love. Think about how many people have learned about Jesus from Saint Matthew! With your family, talk about how you can teach others about Jesus and his love for them. Put your plan into action.

We Pray

A Prayer for Openness to God's Word

Be kind to your servant that I may
    live,
    that I may keep your word.
Open my eyes to see clearly
    the wonders of your law.
Lead me in the path of your
    commandments,
    for that is my delight.
—Psalm 119:17–18, 35

Lesson 1 Review

A **Complete** the following sentences, using words from the box.

1. The living teaching office of the Church is called the _____.

2. The _____ is another name for Sacred Scripture.

3. Sacred Scripture and Sacred _____ must be understood together.

4. The Bible is God's _____ written by human writers.

5. _____ leads us to know God and to obey him.

Tradition

Faith

Bible

Magisterium

Word

B **Fill in** the circle beside the correct answer.

6. The symbol that represents Saint Matthew is _____.

   ○ **an angel**   ○ **a winged lion**   ○ **an open book**

7. The way God makes himself, and his plan for all people, known to us is called _____.

   ○ **faith**   ○ **Divine Revelation**   ○ **Sacred Scripture**

8. Before becoming a follower of Jesus, Saint Matthew was a _____.

   ○ **Roman governor**   ○ **tax collector**   ○ **teacher**

9. The Gospels have a special place in the Bible because they tell us about _____.

   ○ **Jesus**   ○ **Abraham and David**   ○ **the Gospel writers**

10. The writers of the _____ are called the evangelists.

    ○ **Old Testament**   ○ **New Testament**   ○ **Gospels**

I Believe in God the Father

Let Us Pray

Glory to God

Glory to God in the highest,
and on earth peace to people of good will.
We praise you, we bless you,
we adore you, we glorify you,
we give you thanks
for your great glory,
Lord God, heavenly King,
O God, almighty Father.

— *Roman Missal*

My Catholic Faith

God is our loving Father. He cares for all our needs.

➡ **How can you talk to God as your loving Father? What would you say to him?**

Sacred Scripture

In the Gospel of John, we read about Jesus traveling to Jerusalem for the feast of Passover. When he arrived in Jerusalem, Jesus went to the Temple. He was troubled at what he saw there. Jesus became angry with the people who were disrespecting the Temple. When Jesus spoke to them, he called the Temple his Father's house. This is one of the many times in the Gospels when Jesus calls God his Father.

Jesus Cleanses the Temple

Since the Passover of the Jews was near, Jesus went up to Jerusalem. He found in the temple area those who sold oxen, sheep, and doves, as well as the money-changers seated there. He made a whip out of cords and drove them all out of the temple area, with the sheep and oxen, and spilled the coins of the money-changers and overturned their tables, and to those who sold doves he said, "Take these out of here, and stop making my Father's house a marketplace."

—John 2:13–16

More Scripture on God the Father

You can read more about God the Father in your Bible. Here are some passages:

➡ The Vine and the Branches – John 15:1–10

➡ Last Supper Discourse – John 14:1–14

➡ Jesus Praises the Father – Matthew 11:25–27

Living the Scripture

Create a poster that proclaims that God is our Father and that his house must be treated with respect. Then write a prayer to God the Father.

Father in Heaven,

_____

_____

_____

_____

Our Catholic Tradition

God Is Our Loving Father

God the Father is the First Person of the **Blessed Trinity**. The Blessed Trinity is the mystery of the one God in three Divine Persons. God is our loving Creator. He created the world to show how much he loves us. His love for us will last forever. Creation helps us know God's goodness and his greatness.

In the Old Testament, God gradually made himself known to us in his actions and his words. He also made himself known through the **covenants**, or promises, he made with Adam and Eve, our first parents, and with Noah and Abraham. But it was through Jesus, his only Son, that God made himself fully known to us.

Remember learning about Noah, Abraham, and Moses in the first chapter? They helped the people of the Old Testament believe that God is the one true God. But Jesus taught us much more about God. He taught us that God is a loving Father who looks after all our needs. Jesus also promised us that God would send the Holy Spirit to guide us. The Holy Spirit guides the Church to do God's will. God the Father, God the Son, and God the Holy Spirit are the one God in three Divine Persons.

The mystery of the Blessed Trinity is something we cannot understand completely. It is the most important mystery of our Christian faith.

Who is the Blessed Trinity?

How did God make himself known to us?

What did Jesus teach us about God?

Live Your Faith

Find the hidden words about God the Father and the Blessed Trinity.

Father	Creator	First Person	Son
Trinity	mystery	Holy Spirit	love

V	Y	O	P	F	U	Y	I	N	K	T
B	R	C	S	I	B	H	O	V	E	S
E	J	N	H	R	O	S	D	D	W	Z
D	F	T	O	S	E	F	P	C	D	Y
Z	A	R	L	T	B	F	W	R	C	D
Y	T	I	Y	P	M	L	Y	E	N	Z
I	H	N	S	E	Y	O	Z	A	J	Q
P	E	I	P	R	S	V	T	T	T	D
O	R	T	I	S	T	E	E	O	M	K
Z	M	Y	R	O	E	U	P	R	D	J
D	E	R	I	N	R	I	B	P	B	M
I	W	R	T	M	Y	K	D	T	T	S

Choose two of the words you found and use them in a sentence about God the Father.

_____

_____

_____

FAITH FACTS

➡ God created the universe because of his love for us. He created us to share in his truth, goodness, and beauty.

➡ Although God the Father is identified with the work of creation, the three Divine Persons of the Trinity—Father, Son, and Holy Spirit—are together the source of all creation.

➡ God created us to live in happiness with him in this life and in Heaven.

Words to Know

Blessed Trinity
one God in three Divine Persons—God the Father, God the Son, and God the Holy Spirit

covenant
a sacred promise or agreement between God and humans, such as the covenants he made with Noah and Abraham

Saints and Holy People

Saint Hilda of Whitby (614–680)

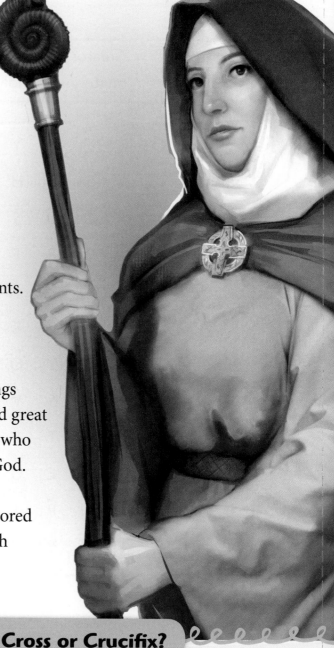

Saint Hilda of Whitby was a princess who lived in England. She lived a life of comfort in her family's palace. She was baptized into the Christian faith at age thirteen.

When Hilda was thirty-three years old, she decided to dedicate her life to God. She became a nun. Hilda was put in charge of a double monastery for monks and nuns in the north of England. In 657, Hilda founded her own monastery at Whitby. The monastery drew many men and women who wanted to dedicate their lives to God. Five men from the monastery later became bishops and two are now saints.

Saint Hilda believed it was important to learn about God from the Bible. Everyone who joined her monastery had to study Scripture every day.

Hilda developed a reputation for wisdom, and kings and princes came to her for advice. Hilda also showed great care for ordinary people. She encouraged a shepherd who worked at the monastery to write songs of praise to God. This shepherd became an important English poet.

Because of her love of learning, Saint Hilda is honored as the patroness of education and culture. The Church celebrates her feast day on November 17.

Catholic Customs — Cross or Crucifix?

Do you know the difference between a cross and crucifix? A cross depicts the simple beams that Jesus hung on. A crucifix is a cross with a corpus, or a sculpture or image of Jesus' body. A crucifix helps us remember Jesus' death for us. Most Catholic churches have a crucifix above the altar. The next time you are in church, look for a crucifix, either above the altar or in another part of the church.

Make It Happen

Saint Hilda believed it was important to learn about God by reading the Bible. In the space below, write a note to a family member or friend telling why the Bible is important. Tell the person how the Bible can help him or her know about God.

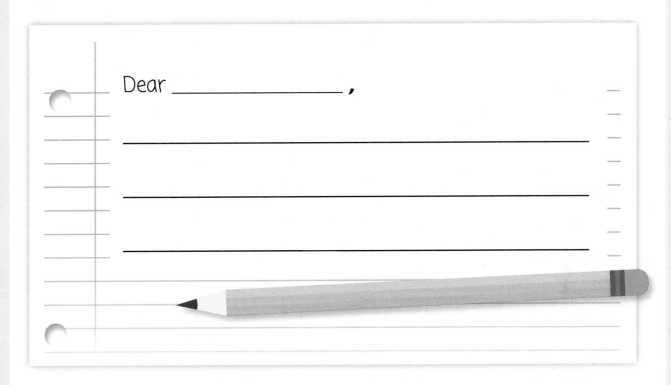

Dear _____ ,

Reach Out!

Think of someone you know with a special talent, such as in music or art.
➡ **How can you encourage this person to use this talent to honor God?**

We Pray
Act of Faith

O God, we firmly believe that you are one God in three Divine Persons, Father, Son and Holy Spirit; we believe that your Divine Son became man and died for our sins, and that he will come to judge the living and the dead. We believe these and all the truths that the Holy Catholic Church teaches, because you have revealed them, and you can neither deceive nor be deceived. Amen.

Lesson 2 Review

A **Complete** the following sentences, using words from the box.

1. _____ is the mystery of the one God in three Divine Persons.

2. _____ is the First Person of the Blessed Trinity.

3. We can know God's goodness and his greatness through _____ .

4. _____ taught us that God is a loving Father.

5. The Church honors _____ as the patroness of education.

Creation
Saint Hilda of Whitby
The Blessed Trinity
God the Father
Jesus

B **Fill in** the circle beside the correct answer.

6. A _____ is a sacred agreement between God and humans.
   ○ **covenant**   ○ **mystery**   ○ **promise**

7. Saint Hilda wanted all the members of her monastery to study _____ .
   ○ **music**   ○ **poetry**   ○ **the Bible**

8. Jesus called the _____ in Jerusalem his Father's house.
   ○ **Temple**   ○ **ark**   ○ **Passover**

9. God created us to live _____ with him.
   ○ **on earth**   ○ **in happiness**   ○ **alone**

10. In the Old Testament, God gradually made himself known through his words and _____ .
   ○ **teachings**   ○ **deeds**   ○ **promises**

I Believe in Jesus Christ

Let Us Pray

A Blessing Prayer

Leader: Loving God, we thank you for sending your Son, Jesus, into the world to save us.

All: We thank you and we bless you, Lord.

Leader: Loving God, through your Son, Jesus Christ, we can have eternal life.

All: We thank you and we bless you, Lord.

Leader: Loving God, you have chosen us to be your people. Open our hearts to your love and mercy.

All: We thank you and we bless you, Lord.

My Catholic Faith

Through Jesus' death on the Cross we can live forever with God.

 How does knowing this make you feel?

Sacred Scripture

Before Jesus began teaching in public and calling his disciples, a **prophet** named Saint John the Baptist told people to prepare for Jesus' coming. He told them to be baptized so they can be forgiven of their sins. People traveled to the Jordan River to be baptized by John. Although Jesus did not need to be baptized, he went to John to be baptized, too.

The Baptism of Jesus

Now the people were filled with expectation, and all were asking in their hearts if John might be the Messiah. John answered them all, saying, "I am baptizing you with water, but one mightier than I is coming. I am not worthy to loosen the thongs of his sandals. He will baptize you with the holy Spirit and fire."

After all the people had been baptized and Jesus also had been baptized and was praying, heaven was opened and the holy Spirit descended upon him in bodily form like a dove. And a voice came from heaven, "You are my beloved Son; with you I am well pleased."

—Luke 3:15–16, 21–22

Scripture at Mass

The Scripture passage about Jesus' Baptism is read at Mass on the Feast of the Baptism of the Lord. The Church celebrates this feast day during the Christmas season.

Living the Scripture

Tell how Saint John the Baptist helped other people know about Jesus.

_____

_____

You can help others know about Jesus, too. Describe two ways you can make Jesus known through your words or actions.

1. _____

_____

2. _____

_____

Words to Know

prophet
a person God has chosen to speak in his name

Our Catholic Tradition

Jesus, the Son of God

What does the term "good news" mean to you? What are some times you remember receiving extra special good news?

As a follower of Jesus you have heard the most important good news of all: the Good News of Jesus. This Good News begins with the **Incarnation**, when Jesus Christ became man.

Because of his love for all people, God the Father sent his Son, Jesus, into the world. Through the power of the Holy Spirit, Jesus was born of the Virgin Mary. Jesus is the Son of God and the Second Person of the Blessed Trinity. For all eternity, Jesus is the only Son of the Father and also God himself. Because of this, he is the mediator between us and God.

Jesus is a sign of God's love for all people. He shows us the way to live in happiness with God. Everything he taught us and did while he was on earth helps us understand God's love.

Jesus especially made God's love known to us through his suffering and his death on the Cross, and his glorious **Resurrection** and **Ascension**. These events are known as the **Paschal Mystery**.

What is the Incarnation?

Why did God send Jesus into the world?

What is the Paschal Mystery?

Live Your Faith

Write a prayer to Jesus by completing the following sentences. In the round frame in the corner, draw a symbol of your faith in Jesus.

Lord Jesus, _____

_____

I believe _____

_____.

Help me _____

_____.

Lead me _____

_____.

I praise and thank you for

_____

_____.

Amen.

FAITH FACTS

➡ Jesus Christ is truly God and truly man. He is divine and human.

➡ We call Jesus the Messiah. The word *Messiah* is Hebrew for "anointed one." Jesus is the anointed one because God chose him to save us from sin.

Words to Know

Incarnation
the mystery that the Son of God took on a human nature to save all people

Resurrection
Jesus being raised from the dead three days after his death on the Cross

Ascension
when the Risen Jesus was taken up to Heaven to be with God the Father forever

Paschal Mystery
the suffering, death, Resurrection, and Ascension of Jesus

Saints and Holy People

Saint Anthony of Padua (1195–1231)

Saint Anthony of Padua was born to a noble family in Portugal. At age fifteen, Anthony joined the Augustinians, an order of religious priests and brothers. Later, after becoming a priest, he joined the Franciscan order. He hoped to travel to North Africa to preach the Gospel.

On his way to Africa, Anthony became very ill. He was taken to Italy to rest and get better. One day while he was in Italy, he was invited to give the homily at Mass. To his own and everyone's amazement, Anthony was a wonderful preacher. All the people gathered were inspired by his words.

From then on Anthony began to preach in public, especially in Padua. He would speak to people gathered in the streets about the love of God and the Good News of Jesus. By his words and example, Anthony helped many people believe in the Gospel message.

Saint Anthony had great love for Jesus. He taught about the wonder of Jesus' Incarnation. Once when he was praying, a brilliant light filled his room. Jesus then appeared to Saint Anthony in the form of a little child.

According to legend, when Saint Anthony died angels rang church bells throughout his city. We celebrate Saint Anthony's feast day on June 13.

Catholic Customs   The Franciscans

The Franciscan Order of religious was founded by Saint Francis of Assisi (1182–1226). Saint Francis wanted his followers to live a life of simplicity and poverty. He wanted them to serve the poor and preach the Gospel.

Franciscans live according to the Rule of Saint Francis. Here is a small portion of the Rule: I counsel ... my brothers in the Lord Jesus Christ that ... they shall be gentle, ... mild and humble, and virtuous in speech.

Make It Happen

Draw a picture about a time when you taught others about God and his love, either through your words or through something you did. Add a caption to your drawing.

Faith at Home

Saint Anthony of Padua had a gift for preaching. He used it to teach others about God's love. As a family, talk about a special gift or talent each person in the family has. Make a plan for each family member to use his or her special gift to bring God's love to at least one other person this week.

We Pray

A Prayer to Jesus

O most merciful Redeemer, Friend, and Brother,
may I know you more clearly,
love you more dearly,
and follow you more nearly,
for ever and ever. Amen.

— Based on a prayer by Saint
Richard of Chichester

Lesson 3 Review

A **Match** each term in column B with its definition in column A by writing the correct letter in the space provided.

Column A

1. _____ a Hebrew word that means "anointed one"

2. _____ the mystery that the Son of God became man to save all people

3. _____ the suffering, death, Resurrection, and Ascension of Jesus Christ

4. _____ a person God has chosen to speak in his name

5. _____ when the Risen Jesus was taken up to Heaven to be with God the Father forever

Column B

a. Incarnation

b. Ascension

c. Paschal Mystery

d. Messiah

e. prophet

B **Fill in** the circle beside the correct answer.

6. Jesus is the _____ Divine Person of the Blessed Trinity.
   ○ **First**　　　　　○ **Second**

7. Jesus was baptized by _____.
   ○ **Saint John the Baptist**　　　○ **Saint Anthony of Padua**

8. Saint _____ used his gift of preaching to tell others about God.
   ○ **Anthony of Padua**　　　○ **Francis of Assisi**

9. Jesus Christ is truly _____ and truly man.
   ○ **God**　　　　　○ **good**

10. The _____ is Jesus being raised from the dead three days after his death on the Cross.
    ○ **Ascension**　　　○ **Resurrection**

I Believe in the Holy Spirit

Let Us Pray

The Apostles' Creed

I believe in God,
the Father almighty,
Creator of heaven and earth,
and in Jesus Christ, his only Son, our Lord,
who was conceived by the Holy Spirit,
born of the Virgin Mary,
suffered under Pontius Pilate,
was crucified, died and was buried;
he descended into hell;
on the third day he rose again from the dead;
he ascended into heaven,
and is seated at the right hand of God the Father
almighty; from there he will come to judge the
living and the dead.
I believe in the Holy Spirit,
the holy catholic Church,
the communion of Saints,
the forgiveness of sins,
the resurrection of the body,
and life everlasting. Amen.

— *Roman Missal*

My Catholic Faith

The Apostles' Creed is a summary of our Catholic beliefs.

➠ **What does it mean to you when you express these beliefs?**

Sacred Scripture

When the time came for Jesus' Ascension into Heaven, the Apostles were gathered with him. Jesus promised them that they would receive the power of the Holy Spirit. The Holy Spirit would help them bring the Good News of Jesus' love to all people.

The following words from Scripture tell how this promise became real at **Pentecost**.

More Scripture on the Holy Spirit

You can read more about the Holy Spirit in your Bible. Here are some passages:

➡ God Guides the Israelites out of Egypt — Exodus 13:21

➡ The Preaching of John the Baptist — Matthew 3:11

➡ Jesus Appears to the Apostles — John 20:19–23

The Coming of the Holy Spirit

When the time for Pentecost was fulfilled, they were all in one place together. And suddenly there came from the sky a noise like a strong driving wind, and it filled the entire house in which they were. Then there appeared to them tongues as of fire, which parted and came to rest on each one of them. And they were all filled with the holy Spirit and began to speak in different tongues, as the Spirit enabled them to proclaim.

Now there were devout Jews from every nation under heaven staying in Jerusalem. At this sound, they gathered in a large crowd, but they were confused because each one heard them speaking in his own language. They were astounded and in amazement they asked, "Are not all these people who are speaking Galileans? Then how does each of us hear them in his own native language?"

—Acts 2:1–11

Living the Scripture

When the Apostles received the Holy Spirit, something amazing happened. When they spoke, each person heard them in his or her own language.

Have you ever had trouble explaining something you felt strongly about? Give an example.

_____

_____

How can the Holy Spirit help you talk at times like these?

_____

_____

How can the Holy Spirit help you share with others what you know about God?

_____

_____

Our Catholic Tradition

The Holy Spirit Shares Jesus' Mission

In the story of the Incarnation in the Bible, we learn that Mary conceived Jesus by the power of the Holy Spirit. Through Mary, the Holy Spirit made it possible for Jesus to come into the world. We can see the Holy Spirit at work in both the Old Testament and the New Testament. For example, in the Old Testament, when God created the world, the Holy Spirit appeared as a mighty wind. In the New Testament, the Holy Spirit is present at Jesus' Baptism. Here, the Holy Spirit appears as a dove. Later in the Gospels, Jesus promises his disciples that the Father will send the Holy Spirit to be with them always. As you read in the Scripture about the coming of the Holy Spirit, this promise was fulfilled on Pentecost. On that day, the Holy Spirit came to the Apostles and to the Virgin Mary.

Pentecost marks the day the work of the Church began. On Pentecost, the Apostles were able to begin their work of **evangelization**. Today, the Holy Spirit continues to help the Church and make her holy.

The Holy Spirit is the Third Divine Person of the Blessed Trinity. The role of the Holy Spirit is united with the role of Jesus. Together they strengthen the Church and make her holy.

Where do we see the Holy Spirit at work in the Bible?

Why did the Church begin to grow at Pentecost?

Live Your Faith

Design and decorate a bookmark about Pentecost. Be sure to include a symbol for the Holy Spirit and a message about what happened at Pentecost.

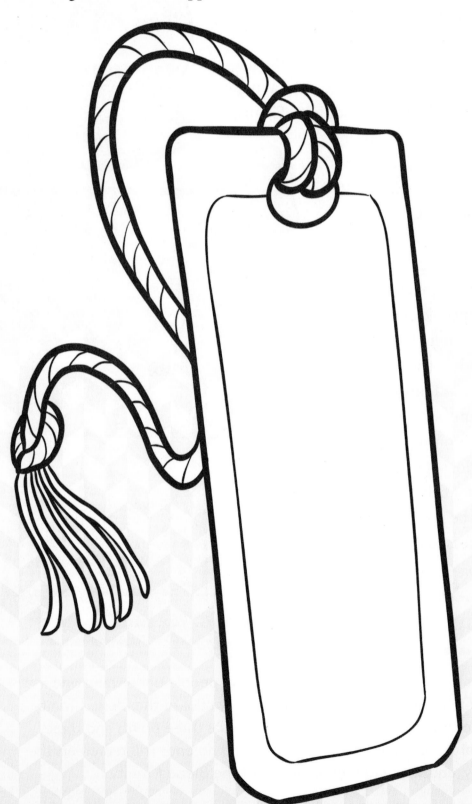

Words to Know

evangelization sharing the Good News of Jesus through words and actions in a way that invites people to accept the Gospel

Saints and Holy People

Saint Patrick (c. 387–460)

Saint Patrick was the son of a Roman official in Britain. One day, while tending sheep on his father's farm, he was kidnapped by a group of pirates and sold as a slave.

Patrick was taken to Ireland. He was forced to work on a farm, and had little to eat and no warm place to sleep at night. For six years Patrick lived in these harsh conditions. Finally, he was able to escape and return to his family.

When he was back home in Britain, Patrick often thought about the people of Ireland. He wanted to help them know about God's love and about Jesus.

Patrick prepared to become a priest. In time, he became a bishop and returned to Ireland. Patrick helped the people of Ireland learn about God. He taught them about the Blessed Trinity. According to legend, Patrick helped the people understand the mystery of the Trinity by comparing it to a shamrock. Just as the shamrock is one clover but has three leaves, so the Trinity is one God in three Divine Persons: Father, Son, and Holy Spirit.

Saint Patrick is known for bringing the Christian faith to Ireland. Because of this, he is the patron saint of Ireland. The Church celebrates his feast day on March 17.

Catholic Customs   The Triqueta: A Symbol for the Trinity

Saint Patrick used the shamrock to help people understand one God in three Divine Persons. Another symbol of the Blessed Trinity is the triqueta (tri KE ta). The triqueta has three points and three equal sides, and it has no beginning and no end. This represents the unity, equality, and eternal nature of the Blessed Trinity.

Make It Happen

Saint Patrick used a shamrock to help people understand one God in three Divine Persons. Label each of the spaces below for each Divine Person of the Trinity. Then in each space, write or draw one thing you know about that Divine Person.

Reach Out!

Saint Patrick taught the people of Ireland about the Christian faith.

➡ **Whom can you teach about your faith? How can you do so?**

We Pray

Glory Be

Glory be to the Father
and to the Son
and to the Holy Spirit
as it was in the beginning
is now, and ever shall be
world without end.
Amen.

A **Complete** the crossword puzzle using the following clues.

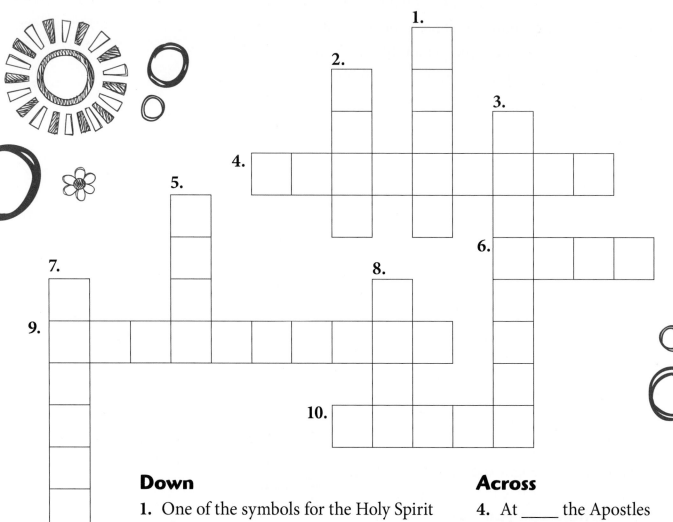

Down

1. One of the symbols for the Holy Spirit that is used at Baptism is ____.

2. In the Old Testament, when God created the world, the Holy Spirit appeared as ____.

3. Proclaiming the ____ of Jesus and the love of God is called evangelization.

5. ____ was present with the Apostles at Pentecost.

7. Saint Patrick used a ____ to explain the mystery of the Blessed Trinity.

8. At Pentecost the Holy Spirit came in the form of tongues of ____.

Across

4. At ____ the Apostles began their work of evangelization.

6. At Jesus' Baptism the Holy Spirit appeared in the form of a ____.

9. The ____ is the Third Divine Person of the Blessed Trinity.

10. Mary conceived ____ by the power of the Holy Spirit.

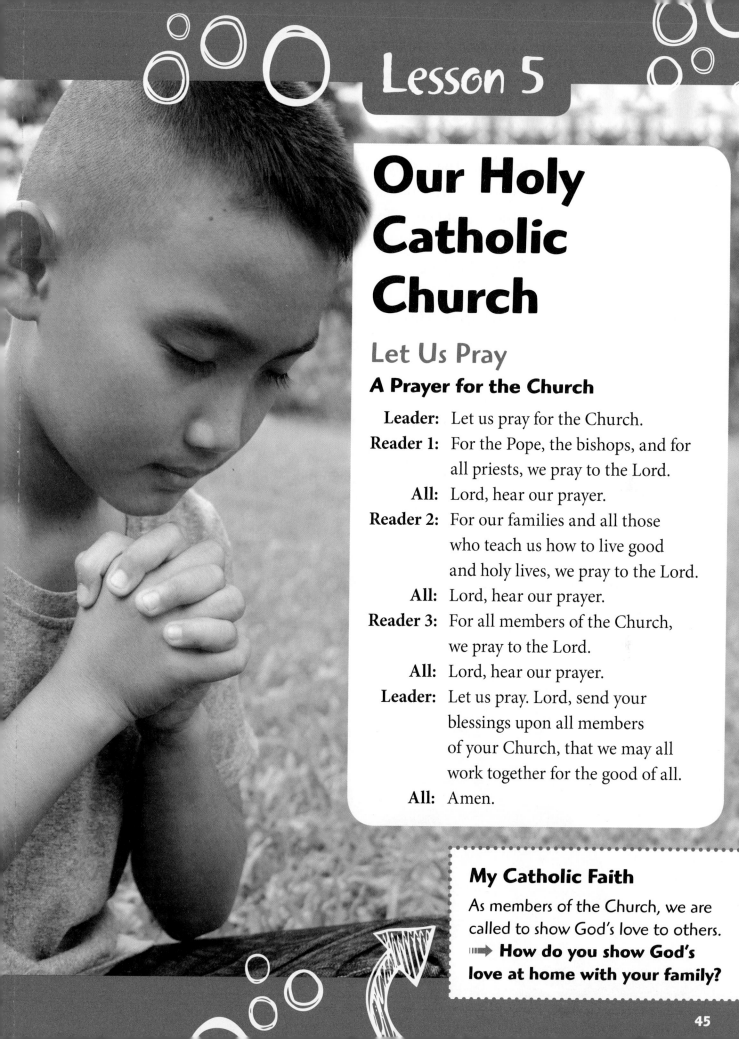

Our Holy Catholic Church

Let Us Pray

A Prayer for the Church

Leader: Let us pray for the Church.

Reader 1: For the Pope, the bishops, and for all priests, we pray to the Lord.

All: Lord, hear our prayer.

Reader 2: For our families and all those who teach us how to live good and holy lives, we pray to the Lord.

All: Lord, hear our prayer.

Reader 3: For all members of the Church, we pray to the Lord.

All: Lord, hear our prayer.

Leader: Let us pray. Lord, send your blessings upon all members of your Church, that we may all work together for the good of all.

All: Amen.

My Catholic Faith

As members of the Church, we are called to show God's love to others.
➠ **How do you show God's love at home with your family?**

Sacred Scripture

Did you know that the Catholic Church is both visible and invisible? The visible part of the Church is what we can experience with our senses. This includes things like the gathering of people for Mass and prayers we hear and say. The invisible, or spiritual, part is the way the Church shares Christ's love. Because of this we say that the Church is both human and divine. Jesus established the Church when he was on earth. He chose the Apostles to be the leaders of the Church. He chose Saint Peter as the leader of the Apostles and of the Church.

Scripture at Mass

This reading from the Gospel of Matthew reminds us of the responsibility Jesus gave the Pope to lead the Church on earth. It is read at Mass on February 22, the Feast of the Chair of Saint Peter the Apostle. This feast honors the Pope and his ministry.

Jesus Calls Peter to Lead the Church

[Jesus] asked his disciples, "Who do people say that the Son of Man is?" They replied, "Some say John the Baptist, others Elijah, still others Jeremiah or one of the prophets." He said to them, "But who do you say that I am?" Simon Peter said in reply, "You are the Messiah, the Son of the living God."

Jesus said to him in reply, "Blessed are you, Simon.... For flesh and blood has not revealed this to you, but my heavenly Father. And so I say to you, you are Peter, and upon this rock I will build my church.... I will give you the keys to the kingdom of heaven. Whatever you bind on earth shall be bound in heaven. Whatever you loose on earth will be loosed in heaven."

—Matthew 16:13–20

Living the Scripture

Suppose Jesus asked you, "Who do you say I am?" How would you answer?
Write your response.

_____

_____

_____

_____

You can express your beliefs about Jesus through your words and through your
actions. In the space below, write three ways you can share what you believe through
words. Then write three ways you can show what you believe through your actions.

Through my words	Through my actions

Our Catholic Tradition

Jesus Founded the Church

In the earliest days after Jesus' Ascension, the Church was centered in Jerusalem. Small groups of Christians gathered for worship in one another's homes. As the disciples taught the Gospel message to more and more people, the Church grew. Christianity was established in new places. Today the Catholic Church includes people from all over the world. The Pope and the bishops lead Christ's Church on earth.

The Church is an assembly of the People of God. Her unity flows from the unity of the Blessed Trinity. We call the Church the **Body of Christ**. Like a body the Church is one but is made up of many parts, or members. Through the Holy Spirit, Christ bestows on the Church four marks: one, holy, catholic, and apostolic. These qualities are called the Marks of the Church. Christ calls on the Church to live and make real these special qualities.

> How has the Church grown over time?

> Why do we call the Church the Body of Christ?

The Marks of the Church	
one	The Church is *one* because she was founded by Jesus Christ, and is united by the Holy Spirit in one faith.
holy	The Church is *holy* because she is united with Christ and made holy by him. The Church is holy to be a sign of Christ's presence in the world.
catholic	The word *catholic* means universal, or for all people. The Church is universal because she was sent by Christ to bring the Good News to all people.
apostolic	The Church is *apostolic* because Jesus began the Church with the Apostles. The Church today teaches what the Apostles taught, and is led by them through the Pope and the bishops.

Live Your Faith

Fill in the blanks to show how you belong to the universal Church. Then tell why belonging to the Church is important to you.

My name is _____

The parish I belong to is _____

_____

My parish is in the diocese of _____

Our bishop is _____

The name of the Pope is _____

It is important to me to belong to the Catholic Church because _____

_____

_____

Words to Know

Body of Christ
A name for the Church. Christ is the head of the Church, and all the baptized are members of the Body.

papal infallibility
the gift of the Holy Spirit given to the Pope and the bishops in union with him to teach about faith and morals without error

Saints and Holy People

Saint Peter (first century)

Saint Peter was one of the Twelve Apostles. Peter showed great faith in Jesus. When Jesus asked the Apostles to tell who he was, Peter knew Jesus was the Messiah. Because of this Jesus said to him, "You are Peter, and upon this rock I will build my Church" (Matthew 16:18). This meant that Jesus was making Peter the leader of his Church on earth.

Saint Peter was the first Pope. Another name for the Pope is the Vicar of Christ. When Rome became the center of the Church, Saint Peter also became the bishop of Rome. All the Popes since Saint Peter carry on the mission of leading the Church.

Pope Francis (1936–)

Pope Francis is the 266th Pope to follow Saint Peter. Before becoming Pope, he was a bishop and then a cardinal from Argentina. He is the first Pope from Latin America.

Before becoming Pope, Francis was known as Cardinal Jorge Mario Bergoglio. He chose the name Francis in honor of Saint Francis of Assisi. Saint Francis gave up worldly riches to serve God and the poor. Pope Francis has been helping Catholics and all people understand that it is important to take care of people in need.

Catholic Customs   The Pope Travels to Share the Gospel

One of the Pope's responsibilities is to teach about God's love. In recent times, popes have traveled to different countries to teach about God. Pope Saint John Paul II (1978–2005) traveled to more than one hundred countries. He made seven visits to the United States. Pope Francis also travels to spread the Gospel message. Not long after he became Pope, Pope Francis traveled to Brazil for World Youth Day. Nearly three million young people gathered to hear him speak and to celebrate Mass.

Make It Happen

What do you think is most different about being Pope in the first century—around the time of the Early Church—and today? What do you think is the same? In the chart below, write some things that are different, and some that are the same.

Different

The Same

Faith at Home

As a family, talk about our current Pope and some of the things he has taught about loving others. Together pray for the Pope and all the bishops. Ask God to bless them and guide them always in leading his Church.

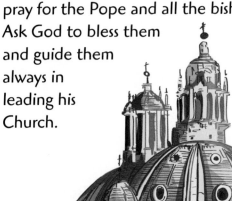

We Pray

A Prayer for the Pope

O God, Pastor and Ruler of all the faithful, look upon your servant, Pope Francis, whom you have appointed to preside over your Church. Grant that by word and example, he may teach all those under his care. With the flock entrusted to him, may he share in life everlasting. We ask this through Christ our Lord. Amen.

—Based on the *Roman Missal*

Lesson 5 Review

A Match each Mark of the Church in column B with its meaning in column A by writing the letter in the space provided.

Column A

1. _____ The Church is universal, because Jesus sent the Church out to bring the Good News of salvation to all people.

2. _____ The Church is united with God and called by God for a specific purpose.

3. _____ The Holy Spirit unites all the members of the Church in faith.

4. _____ The Church today teaches what the Apostles taught, and is led by them through the Pope and the bishops.

Column B

a. one

b. holy

c. catholic

d. apostolic

B Fill in the circle beside the correct answer.

5. The authority and power to lead and teach the Church is passed down from the Apostles to the Pope and bishops. This is called _____.

   ○ **Apostolic Succession**   ○ **papal infallibility**

6. With the help of the Holy Spirit, the Pope and the bishops teach about faith and morals without error. This is called _____.

   ○ **Apostolic Succession**   ○ **papal infallibility**

7. When Jesus called Saint Peter to be the leader of the Church, he called him _____.
   ○ **the Vicar of Christ**   ○ **the rock**

8. Another name for the Pope is _____.
   ○ **the Vicar of Christ**   ○ **the rock**

9. Saint _____ was the first Pope.
   ○ **Francis**   ○ **Peter**

10. Before _____ became Pope, he was known as Cardinal Jorge Mario Bergoglio.
    ○ **Pope Francis**   ○ **Saint Peter**

Mary, the Mother of God

Let Us Pray

Hail Holy Queen

Leader: Let us join together and pray this prayer honoring Mary.

All: Hail, Holy Queen, Mother of Mercy, our life, our sweetness, and our hope!
To you do we cry,
poor banished children of Eve;
to you do we send up our sighs,
mourning and weeping in this vale of tears.
Turn, then, most gracious advocate,
your eyes of mercy toward us;
and after this our exile,
show to us the blessed fruit of your womb, Jesus.
O clement, O loving, O sweet Virgin Mary!

My Catholic Faith

When God asked Mary to be the Mother of Jesus, she said yes.
➡ **When do you say yes to God?**

Sacred Scripture

In the Gospel of Luke, we read about the angel Gabriel's visit to Mary. At this visit, Gabriel told Mary that God had chosen her to be the Mother of his Son, Jesus. This event is called the **Annunciation**. Soon after, Mary went to visit her cousin Elizabeth. Elizabeth was also expecting a baby. The Gospel of Luke tells us about this visit.

Mary Visits Her Cousin Elizabeth

When Elizabeth heard Mary's greeting, the infant leaped in her womb, and Elizabeth, filled with the holy Spirit, cried out in a loud voice and said, "Most blessed are you among women, and blessed is the fruit of your womb. And how does this happen to me that the mother of my Lord should come to me? For at the moment the sound of your greeting reached my ears, the infant in my womb leaped for joy. Blessed are you who believed that what was spoken to you by the Lord would be fulfilled."

And Mary said:

"My soul proclaims the greatness of the Lord,
my spirit rejoices in God my savior....

From now on will all ages call me blessed.

The Mighty One has done great things for me,
and holy is his name."

— Luke 1:41–49

More Scripture on Mary

You can read about Mary in other Scripture passages. Here are some:

⟫ The Annunciation – Luke 1:26–38

⟫ The Birth of Jesus – Luke 2:1–7

⟫ The Presentation of Jesus in the Temple – Luke 2:22–38

Living the Scripture

Put the following events from Scripture in order from 1 to 5 by writing the number on the line. Then, in the space on the right, draw a picture of one of the events. Give your drawing a title.

_____ Mary went to visit her cousin Elizabeth.

_____ Mary spoke words of praise to God.

_____ The baby in Elizabeth's womb leaped for joy.

_____ The angel Gabriel visited Mary to tell her God wanted her to be the Mother of Jesus.

_____ Elizabeth was filled with the Holy Spirit and said Mary was blessed.

_____

Words to Know

Annunciation
the angel Gabriel's announcement to Mary that God had chosen her to be the Mother of Jesus

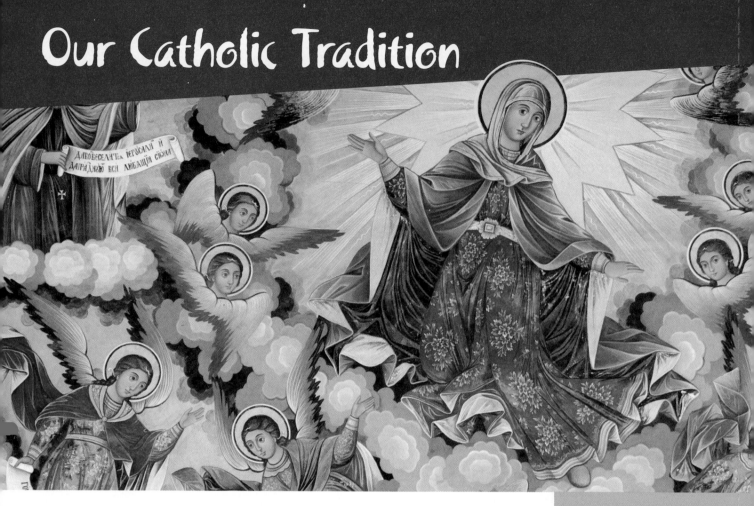

Mary Is the Mother of God

The Virgin Mary had an important role in God's plan for our salvation. God chose her to be the Mother of his Divine Son, Jesus. Because of this, God made Mary free from Original Sin from the moment she was conceived. We call this the **Immaculate Conception**. This means Mary was in a perfect state of grace from the first moment she came into being. She remained free from sin throughout her life.

Jesus Christ was conceived by the power of the Holy Spirit. Mary had no children other than Jesus. Because Mary is the Mother of Jesus, who is also God, she is the Mother of God. Mary is also our spiritual mother. She guides us in following her Son, Jesus.

Because Mary was always faithful to God, at the end of her earthly life she was taken up into Heaven body and soul. This event is called the **Assumption**. We celebrate the Feast of the Assumption on August 15.

What is the Immaculate Conception?

Why do we say Mary is the Mother of God?

What do we celebrate on the Feast of the Assumption?

Live Your Faith

Unscramble the following words about Mary. The first and last letter of each word is done for you.

A I _ _ _ _ _ _ _ _ _ E

I M T U L A M A C E

C O N C E P T I O N

B A _ _ _ _ _ _ _ _ N

A M S U P I O S N T

C A _ _ _ _ _ _ _ _ _ _ N

A U C N N I A T N O I N

D M _ _ _ _ R

M E T R H O

FAITH FACTS

⟹ At the Annunciation, Mary said yes to being the Mother of Jesus. By saying yes, she cooperated with God in the work of salvation.

⟹ Jesus is the Head of the Church. Mary, his Mother, is also the Mother of the Church.

⟹ As the Mother of the Church, Mary continues to help us. She intercedes, or speaks to God, for us. She is an example of faith and love for us.

Now complete each sentence below by putting the letter of the word or words from the list above in the space provided.

1. Mary was free from sin from the moment she came into being. This is called the _____ .

2. God chose Mary to be the _____ of his Son, Jesus.

3. The angel Gabriel's visit to Mary to tell her that God wanted her to be the Mother of his Son is called the _____ .

4. At the end of Mary's earthly life, her body and soul were taken up into Heaven. This is called the _____ .

Words to Know

Immaculate Conception
the truth that God kept Mary free from sin from the first moment she came into being

Assumption
the teaching that after her earthly life, Mary was taken into Heaven, body and soul, to be with God

Saints and Holy People

Saint Dominic Savio (1842–1857)

Dominic Savio was born in a small village in northern Italy. When Dominic was twelve years old, he joined Saint John Bosco as a student at his school in Turin. Dominic founded a group he called the Company of the Immaculate Conception. The boys in this group gathered for prayer and devotion to Mary. They also helped take care of the school and looked after neglected children who enrolled at the school.

Dominic tried hard to please God in everything he did. He would say, "I can't do big things. But I want all I do, even the smallest thing, to be for the greater glory of God."

Dominic hoped to become a priest. But at age fifteen, he developed a lung infection. He was sent home to recover, but his illness grew worse and he died not long after. Just before he died, Dominic described to his father a vision of Heaven.

In 1859, John Bosco chose a group of young men to be the first members of his religious order, the Salesians. All of them had been members of Dominic's Company of the Immaculate Conception.

Dominic Savio was declared a saint in 1954. His feast day is March 9.

Catholic Customs — Titles for Mary

We honor Mary with many different titles. For example, we call Mary the Mother of God and the Blessed Mother. Each title tells us something about who Mary is. Another title for Mary is Queen of Heaven. Calling Mary "Queen" reminds us of her special place in Heaven and of her closeness to Jesus.

Make It Happen

Saint Dominic Savio worked to honor God in all that he did. From his example we can learn to always do what pleases God. Some ways you can do this are to treat others with kindness and to always be honest. Think of one more thing you can do to honor God. Then write a short prayer telling God what you will do.

Dear God, _____

_____

_____

Reach Out!

Saint Dominic Savio helped children who came to his school who didn't have anyone to care for them.

➠ **Who can you help through your words or actions?**

We Pray
The Hail Mary

Hail, Mary, full of grace,
the Lord is with thee.
Blessed art thou among women,
and blessed is the fruit of thy
    womb, Jesus.
Holy Mary, Mother of God,
pray for us sinners,
now and at the hour of our death.
Amen.

A Complete the following sentences, using words from the box.

1. Mary was an important part of God's plan for our

   _____.

2. Because Mary is the Mother of Jesus, who is also God, she is

   is also the Mother of _____.

3. The _____ means
   that Mary was in a perfect state of grace from the first
   moment she came into being.

4. Jesus Christ was conceived by the power of the _____ .

5. Mary is the Mother of Jesus. She is our spiritual Mother and the

   Mother of the _____.

Church
Immaculate Conception
Holy Spirit
God
salvation

B Fill in the circle beside the correct answer.

6. Saint Dominic Savio said, "I want to do all, even the _____ thing, for the glory of God."
   ○ **most important**   ○ **smallest**   ○ **hardest**

7. At the end of her earthly life, Mary was taken up into Heaven body and soul. This
   event is called the _____.
   ○ **Annunciation**   ○ **Assumption**   ○ **Immaculate Conception**

8. Saint Dominic Savio formed a group called the Company of the Immaculate
   Conception in honor of _____.
   ○ **Saint John Bosco**   ○ **Mary**   ○ **the Holy Spirit**

9. The angel Gabriel's visit to Mary is called the _____.
   ○ **Assumption**   ○ **Annunciation**   ○ **Visitation**

10. After learning that she would be the Mother of Jesus, Mary went to visit her
    cousin _____.
    ○ **Elizabeth**   ○ **Zechariah**   ○ **Dominic**

Everlasting Life with God

Let Us Pray

A Prayer of Praise

Leader: Loving Father, we praise your name forever.

Side 1: Your reign is a reign for all ages, your dominion for all generations.

Side 2: My mouth will speak the praises of the LORD; all flesh will bless his holy name forever and ever.

—Psalm 145:13, 21

All: Loving Father, by his death and Resurrection, your Son, Jesus, gave us eternal life. Help us to live in this world in a way that honors your goodness and love. Amen.

My Catholic Faith

Jesus calls each of us to live in a way that shows love for him and others.
➠ **How well have you done that today?**

Sacred Scripture

Jesus often told stories called **parables** as a way to teach his disciples. Jesus' parables help us know about the **Kingdom of God**. In the parable about the judgment of the nations, Jesus taught about what will happen at the **Last Judgment**.

The Judgment of the Nations

Jesus said to his disciples: "When the Son of Man comes in his glory … he will sit upon his glorious throne, and all the nations will be assembled before him. And he will separate them one from another…. He will place the [good people] on

his right and the [others] on his left. Then the king will say to those on his right, 'Come … [i]nherit the kingdom prepared for you…. For I was hungry and you gave me food, I was thirsty and you gave me drink, a stranger

and you welcomed me, naked and you clothed me, ill and you cared for me, in prison and you visited me.' … Then he will say to those on his left, 'Depart from me…. For I was hungry and you gave me no food, I was thirsty and you gave me no drink, a stranger and you gave me no welcome, naked and you gave me no clothing, ill and in prison, and you did not care for me.' Then they will answer and say, 'Lord, when did we see you hungry or thirsty or a stranger or naked or ill or in prison and not minister to your needs?' He will answer them, 'Amen, I say to you, what you did not do for one of these least ones, you did not do for me.' And these will go off to eternal punishment, but the righteous to eternal life."

—Matthew 25:31–46

Scripture at Mass

We hear the Scripture about the Last Judgment at Mass on the Feast of Christ the King. On this feast the Church celebrates Jesus' Second Coming as judge of the world and ruler of all.

Living the Scripture

Jesus said that at the end of our lives, we will be judged on how we have treated others. In the space below, create a sign sharing Jesus' message about how to treat others.

When have you cared for someone in need?

_____

_____

_____

_____

What are some ways you can show more love and care for those in need?

_____

 _____

_____

Words to Know

parable
a short story Jesus told about everyday life to teach something about God

Kingdom of God
the world of love, peace, and justice that is in Heaven and is still being built on earth

Last Judgment
God's final victory over evil that will happen at the end of time. At that time, Christ will return and judge all the living and the dead.

Our Catholic Tradition

We Believe in Everlasting Life

Have you ever read a story or seen a movie where a character you like dies? This probably made you feel sad. Even though death is sad because it is the end of life on earth, it is also the start of a new life.

When Jesus came to earth, he told people that if they believed in him they would have everlasting life. Jesus' own Resurrection is proof that his promise is true. Because of Jesus, we can be with God in Heaven after our death.

When each of us dies, our **soul** will experience a personal judgment. We will be judged on our faith and works. Depending on how we have lived, we will spend eternity with God forever in **Heaven**. Those who do not love God will be separated from him forever in **Hell**.

Of course, most people are not perfectly holy when they die. Because of this, before being with God in Heaven, souls usually have to be purified in **Purgatory**.

At Christ's Second Coming, we will experience the Last Judgment. We believe that because of God's grace our loving actions will lead us to eternal life in Heaven. In Heaven, we will live in happiness with God, with Mary, with the angels and the saints, and with all people who love God.

What does the Church teach about life after death?

What is Purgatory?

What will happen at Jesus' Second Coming?

Live Your Faith

What do you picture when you think about Heaven? Write three words that describe Heaven to you. Then use two of those words to write a short paragraph about what Heaven might be like.

Words about Heaven

_____

_____

_____

What Heaven Might Be Like

_____

_____

_____

_____

_____

_____

FAITH FACTS

➡ When we die, our souls are separated from our bodies. At our resurrection on the last day God will reunite our body with our soul.

➡ At the end of time, the Kingdom of God will be complete. Those who love God will be with him forever, in body and soul.

Words to Know

soul
the spiritual part of a human that lives forever

Heaven
the full joy of living with God forever

Hell
being separated from God forever because of a choice to turn away from him and not ask for forgiveness

Purgatory
a state of final purification after death and before entering into Heaven

Saints and Holy People

Saint Dismas (first century)

You have probably seen images of Jesus' Crucifixion showing two other crosses next to Jesus' Cross. Do you know who is on those crosses? In the Gospel of Luke, we read that two thieves were crucified alongside Jesus. One of those thieves is now known as the Good Thief. We also know him as Saint Dismas.

You can read about Saint Dismas, the Good Thief, in Luke 23:32–43. Luke's Gospel tells us that the two criminals crucified with Jesus acted very differently toward Jesus. One of the criminals insulted him. The other, whom we now know as Saint Dismas, defended Jesus. He knew that Jesus was God. He said to Jesus, "Remember me when you come into your kingdom." Jesus replied, "Today you will be with me in Paradise."

Even though Dismas had been a thief, he asked Jesus for forgiveness. He also believed in Jesus' promise of eternal life. The story of Saint Dismas reminds us of God's mercy. It also tells us that Jesus wants us to live in happiness with God in Heaven.

The Church celebrates the feast of Saint Dismas on March 25.

Catholic Customs   The Alpha and Omega

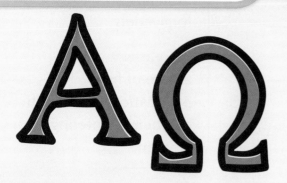

The alpha and omega are the first and last letters of the Greek alphabet. These Greek letters are a symbol for Jesus. In the Book of Revelation, the last book of the New Testament, Jesus is described as the Alpha and the Omega. This tells us that Jesus' presence and his love are eternal.

Make It Happen

The Good Thief asked Jesus to remember him when Jesus comes into his Kingdom. Use the code to find out what Jesus said in reply.

A	B	C	D	E	F	G	H	I	J	K	L	M	N	O	P	Q	R	S	T	U	V	W	X	Y	Z
24				20			17	15						25	21										

___ ___ ___   ___ ___ ___ ___   ___ ___
13 25 7   26 15 1 1   9 20

___ ___ ___ ___   ___ ___
26 15 18 17   16 20

___ ___   ___ ___ ___ ___ ___ ___ ___ ___
15 19   21 24 14 24 2 15 22 20

Faith at Home

The Good Thief was a criminal, but Jesus knew that he was sorry and forgave him. Talk with your family about how Jesus forgives and ways to be more forgiving of one another at home.

We Pray

Act of Hope

O Lord God, I hope by your grace for the pardon of all my sins and after life here to gain eternal happiness because you have promised it who are infinitely more powerful, faithful, kind, and merciful. In this hope I intend to live and die. Amen.

Lesson 7 Review

A **Match** each term in column B with its definition in column A by writing the correct letter in the space provided.

Column A

Column B

1. _____ the spiritual part of a human that lives forever

2. _____ the judgment of all people by Jesus Christ at his Second Coming

3. _____ the full joy of living eternally in God's presence

4. _____ being separated from God forever because of a choice to turn away from him and not seek forgiveness

5. _____ a state of final cleansing after death and before entering into Heaven

a. Purgatory

b. Hell

c. Last Judgment

d. Heaven

e. soul

B **Fill in** the circle beside the correct answer.

6. When we die, we will be judged on our _____ and works.

   ○ faith   ○ words

7. The world of love, peace, and justice that is in Heaven and is still being built on earth is called _____ .

   ○ Purgatory   ○ the Kingdom of God

8. A short story Jesus told about everyday life to teach something about God is called a _____ .

   ○ Scripture   ○ parable

9. Saint Dismas is also known as _____ .

   ○ the Good Thief   ○ the Bad Thief

10. At our _____ on the last day, God will reunite our body with our soul.

    ○ resurrection   ○ Last Judgment

BEING CATHOLIC

God Sent Jesus to Be Our Savior

Because God loves us, he sent Jesus to be our Savior. By accepting death on the Cross, Jesus saved us from sin and made it possible for us to have eternal happiness with God.

Jesus brings us closer to God. By following Jesus' teachings and accepting his love and mercy, we become more holy. This is what happened to a man named Zacchaeus. Zacchaeus was a tax collector who was greedy and unjust. Here is his story.

Jesus was teaching in a town named Jericho. A rich man named Zacchaeus wanted to hear and see Jesus, but the crowd was too large. Zacchaeus ran ahead and climbed a sycamore tree so he could see Jesus when he went by.

When Jesus reached the place where Zacchaeus was, he looked up. Jesus said to Zacchaeus, "Come down quickly. Today I must come to your house."

Zacchaeus joyfully welcomed Jesus into his home. He said to Jesus, "I will give half my possessions to the poor. And if I have stolen from anyone, I will pay him back four times what I stole."

Jesus said, "Today salvation has come to this house."

—Based on Luke 19:1–9

By welcoming Jesus into our hearts, we can also be changed. We can grow in love and in goodness.

Reflect on Change

Write about a time when something you experienced changed you in a good way.

_____

_____

 _____

_____

Who Is Jesus?

Jesus is God's gift of love to us. Jesus is our Teacher, Friend, and Savior.

Jesus teaches us how we should live. In the Sermon on the Mount, Jesus gave us many instructions about the values we should have about life. Jesus also taught us through the many parables, or teaching stories, he told. Another way Jesus taught us is through his example of obeying God and loving others. Jesus also taught us how to pray.

Jesus is our friend. Like a good friend, Jesus always loves and cares for us. Prayer is our way of being friends with Jesus. Jesus always listens to our prayers. Praying is also our way of loving God. When Jesus taught us the Lord's Prayer, he taught us to call God our Father.

Jesus is our Savior. He accepted death on the Cross to save us from sin. He made it possible for us to have eternal happiness with God.

Jesus in My Life

Choose *Teacher, Friend,* or *Savior* as a title for Jesus. Write about how Jesus has that role in your life. Close with a short prayer.

Jesus is my _____

Jesus in my life: _____

_____

_____

Dear God, _____

_____

_____

_____

The Celebration of the Christian Mystery

By the grace of God, Christians ... become temples of the Holy Spirit, living stones out of which the Church is built. (*CCC*, 1197)

71

The Seven Sacraments

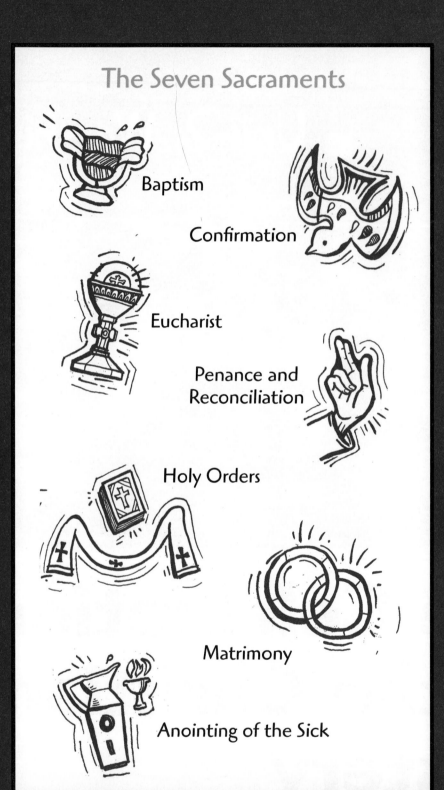

Baptism

Confirmation

Eucharist

Penance and
Reconciliation

Holy Orders

Matrimony

Anointing of the Sick

The Mass

Let Us Pray

The *Sanctus*

Leader: Let us praise Jesus with the words of the *Sanctus*, a prayer from the Mass.

All: Holy, Holy, Holy Lord God of hosts.
Heaven and earth are full of your glory.
Hosanna in the highest.
Blessed is he who comes
in the name of the Lord.
Hosanna in the highest.

— *Roman Missal*

My Catholic Faith

At Mass, we join together in giving thanks and praise to God.

⟫➡ **How well do you know the prayers we pray at Mass? What can you do to know them better?**

73

Sacred Scripture

On the night before Jesus died, he and his disciples gathered to celebrate the Passover. Passover recalls when God led the Israelites out of slavery in Egypt. The night that Jesus celebrated Passover with his disciples is called the **Last Supper**. We call it the Last Supper because it was the last meal Jesus had with his disciples before he died. At the Last Supper, Jesus established the **sacrament** in which he gives us his Body and Blood—the **Sacrament of Eucharist**. This sacrament gives us eternal life with God.

More Scripture on the Eucharist

You can learn more about the Eucharist in your Bible. Here are some passages:

➠ Jesus Feeds Five Thousand — Mark 6:34–42

➠ The Passover — Exodus 12:1–8, 11–14

➠ Jesus, the Bread of Life — John 6:47–51

The Last Supper

When the feast of Passover came, Jesus sent Peter and John to make preparations. They did as Jesus instructed, and prepared a place for Jesus and the Apostles to gather.

When they were gathered at the table, Jesus took the bread. He blessed it and broke it. He gave it to them, saying, "This is my body, which will be given for you. Do this in memory of me."

Jesus then took the cup of wine and said, "This cup is the new covenant in my blood, which will be shed for you."

—Based on Luke 22:7–8, 14–20

Living the Scripture

Choose a phrase that Jesus spoke at the Last Supper and create a banner to display the phrase. Add symbols or other images to your banner.

Words to Know

Last Supper
The meal Jesus shared with his disciples on the night before he died. At the Last Supper, Jesus gave himself in the Eucharist.

sacrament
A special sign and celebration that Jesus gave his Church. The sacraments allow us to share in the life and work of God.

Sacrament of Eucharist
the sacrament in which, through the ministry of the priest and by the power of the Holy Spirit, Jesus shares himself, and the bread and wine become his Body and Blood

Our Catholic Tradition

We Celebrate the Eucharist

At the Last Supper, Jesus gave all people the gift of the Eucharist. Today, we gather at **Mass** to celebrate the Eucharist. Through the Eucharist, we can have eternal life.

At Mass, we give praise and thanks to God for all the gifts he has given us. We especially thank him for the gift of Jesus' Body and Blood in the Eucharist.

At the celebration of the Eucharist, Catholics worship as a community. This kind of public, community worship is called **liturgy**. Although Catholics have many ways to pray and worship, the Eucharist, or the Mass, is the most important. In the Eucharist, we join with Jesus to worship God the Father. Our worship is guided by the Holy Spirit.

At Mass we hear God's Word in Scripture. We profess our faith. We usually do this by praying the Nicene Creed. During the Consecration, when the bread and wine become the Body and Blood of Christ, we recall what Jesus said and did at the Last Supper. We also recall his sacrifice on the Cross. All prayers and actions of the Mass are one act of worship.

Outside of Mass, we can show love for Jesus by visiting the **Blessed Sacrament** in Church. The Blessed Sacrament is another name for the Eucharist, especially the Body of Christ. It is kept in a special place in church called a **Tabernacle**.

When do we gather to celebrate the Eucharist?

What is liturgy?

What happens at Mass?

What is the Blessed Sacrament

Live Your Faith

Write a poem or a prayer giving thanks to God for the gift of the Eucharist. Add a picture to your poem or prayer.

_____

_____

_____

_____

_____

FAITH FACTS

➠ Catholics must attend Mass on Sundays and on Holy Days of Obligation.

➠ Jesus Christ is truly present in the Eucharist.

Words to Know

Mass
the Church's prayer of praise and thanksgiving to God; the celebration of the Eucharist

liturgy
The official public worship of the Church. The Eucharist is the Church's most important liturgy.

Blessed Sacrament
a name for the Holy Eucharist, especially the Body of Christ kept in the Tabernacle

Tabernacle
the special place in church where the Blessed Sacrament is reserved after Mass

Saints and Holy People

Saint Clare of Assisi (1194–1253)

Saint Clare came from a wealthy family in Italy. One day, after she heard Saint Francis of Assisi preach, she decided to live a simple life for Jesus. She shared this wish with Saint Francis. In a little chapel in Assisi, Italy, Saint Francis cut off her hair and gave her a simple brown habit to wear.

Soon other women followed Clare's example. Clare established a religious order for these women. They became known as the Poor Clares. They chose to live a simple life without any possessions. They dedicated their lives to prayer.

Clare and the other nuns were very happy in this life because they knew of God's great love.

Saint Clare had great devotion to Jesus in the Eucharist. When an army came to attack Assisi and the convent where Clare and the sisters lived, Clare prayed to God to protect them. She went to the walls of the convent and placed the Blessed Sacrament in a monstrance where the enemy could see it. Through Jesus' help, the attackers fled without attacking the convent.

We celebrate the feast of Saint Clare on August 11.

Save me o Lord from every Evil of Soul & Body

Catholic Customs Eucharistic Adoration

One way Catholics honor Jesus Christ in the Blessed Sacrament outside of Mass is though Eucharistic Adoration. In this devotion, the Eucharist is placed in a monstrance on the altar. You can see what a monstrance looks like in the picture shown on the left. People sit in Christ's Divine Presence and pray silently. Some parishes have Eucharistic adoration every day. Depending on the scheduled time, this can be called a daily holy hour or perpetual adoration.

Make It Happen

In this chapter you learned about showing devotion to Jesus Christ in the Blessed Sacrament. What are some ways you can do this? In the space below, write or illustrate some of the ways.

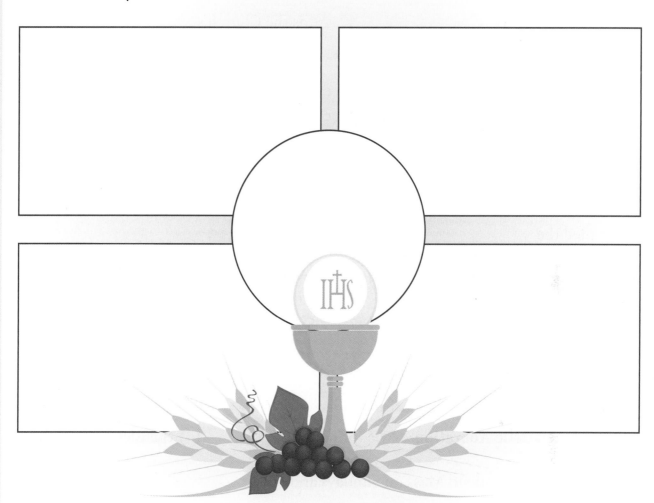

Reach Out!

Saint Clare's devotion to the Blessed Sacrament kept an army from invading her convent and hurting the sisters.

⟶ **Think about one thing you can do today for the good of others with Jesus' help. Make a plan to do it!**

We Pray
A Prayer before the Blessed Sacrament

Lord Jesus, I believe that you are truly present in the Eucharist. As I receive you in Holy Communion, help me to love as you have loved, serve as you have served, so I can be the Body of Christ to others. Amen.

Lesson 8 Review

A Complete the following sentences, using words from the box.

1. On the night before he died, Jesus established the Sacrament of _____ .

2. The _____ is the Church's official public worship.

3. Another name for the Holy Eucharist, especially the Body of Christ kept in the Tabernacle, is the

    _____ .

4. The special place in church where the Blessed Sacrament is reserved after Mass is called the _____ .

5. The meal Jesus shared with his disciples on the night before he died is called the

    _____ .

Blessed Sacrament
Last Supper
liturgy
Tabernacle
Eucharist

B Fill in the circle beside the correct answer.

6. The celebration of the Eucharist is called _____ .
   - ○ Eucharistic Adoration
   - ○ Mass
   - ○ the Blessed Sacrament

7. Catholics must attend Mass on Sundays and on _____.
   - ○ Holy Days of Obligation
   - ○ weekdays
   - ○ holidays

8. The _____ is the Church's most important liturgy.
   - ○ Passover
   - ○ Eucharist
   - ○ Last Supper

9. _____ is a special devotion to Jesus in the Blessed Sacrament.
   - ○ The Tabernacle
   - ○ The liturgy
   - ○ Eucharistic Adoration

10. Saint Clare had a great devotion to _____.
    - ○ Saint Francis
    - ○ the Poor Clares
    - ○ Jesus Christ in the Eucharist

Sacraments of Christian Initiation

Let Us Pray

A Psalm Prayer

Side 1: Shout joyfully to the Lord, all you lands;

Side 2: serve the Lord with gladness; come before him with joyful song.

Side 1: Know that the Lord is God, he made us, we belong to him,

Side 2: we are his people, the flock he shepherds.

All: Good indeed is the Lord, His mercy endures forever, his faithfulness lasts through every generation. Amen.

—Psalm 100:1–3, 5

My Catholic Faith

The psalm you just prayed says to "serve the Lord with gladness."

➡ **What does this mean to you?**

Sacred Scripture

Before his Ascension into Heaven, Jesus gave the Apostles this instruction: "Go, therefore, and make disciples of all nations, baptizing them in the name of the Father, and of the Son, and of the holy Spirit" (Matthew 28:19). The Apostles did as Jesus instructed. In places near and far, they taught about Jesus and baptized new believers. We will read about one of these baptisms.

Philip and the Ethiopian

The Apostle Philip was heading down along the desert route south of Jerusalem. He saw a court official from Ethiopia riding in a chariot. He was on his way to Jerusalem to worship. The Holy Spirit led Philip to go and join the Ethiopian. Philip ran up and heard the man reading from the Hebrew Scriptures. Philip asked him, "Do you understand what you are reading?" The man answered, "How can I unless someone instructs me?" The man invited Philip to join him. He was reading from the writings of the prophet Isaiah. He said to Philip, "About whom is the prophet speaking?" Philip proclaimed the Good News of Jesus to him.

As they traveled along the road, they came to some water. The Ethiopian asked Philip to baptize him. They went down to the water, and Philip baptized him. When they came out of the water, the Ethiopian went on his way rejoicing.

—Based on Acts 8:26–39

Scripture in the Mass

The Scripture about Philip and the Ethiopian is from a book of the Bible called Acts of the Apostles. We often hear passages from Acts of the Apostles during the Second Reading at Mass.

Living the Scripture

Think about the two characters in the Scripture story about Philip and the Ethiopian. Compare yourself to the characters. Which one are you most like in your life as a Christian? Explain why.

_____

_____

_____

Who can you ask important questions about your Catholic faith?

_____

Write a note to this person asking him or her to teach you about Jesus and about your faith.

Dear _____ ,

_____

_____

_____

_____

_____

Our Catholic Tradition

New Life in Christ

What are some groups you belong to? Some groups you name might be your family, your class, your school, a team you are a part of, and the town or city you live in. Another group you belong to is the Catholic Church. The **Sacraments of Christian Initiation** mark your membership in the Church. Through these sacraments you begin a relationship with Christ.

The Sacraments of Christian Initiation are Baptism, Eucharist, and Confirmation. They are essential for our lives as Christians. Baptism is the first sacrament that joins us to Christ. In Baptism, you receive **grace** from God. The gift of

grace helps you live as a follower of Christ. You are also forgiven of **Original Sin** and all sin, and you receive the Holy Spirit.

The Sacraments of Eucharist and Confirmation complete your initiation into the Church. Confirmation anoints us with the Holy Spirit. It also makes the grace we received at Baptism complete. In Confirmation we receive the gifts of the Holy Spirit. This sacrament also makes our relationship with Jesus stronger and helps us live as his disciples.

When you receive the Eucharist, or Holy Communion, you are united with Jesus. You are also forgiven of venial sins, or minor sins. The Eucharist also helps you avoid sin. We must not receive Holy Communion if we are not in a state of grace. This means we must be forgiven of serious sins, or mortal sin, in Confession before receiving the sacrament.

Which sacraments begin our relationship with Christ?

Which sacrament first joins us to Christ?

Which sacrament completes Baptism?

What happens when we receive the Eucharist?

Live Your Faith

Have you ever attended a friend's or family member's Baptism, Confirmation, or First Holy Communion? For each sacrament you have attended, write two things you remember from the liturgy.

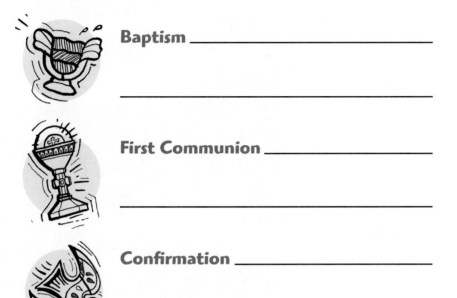

Baptism _____

_____

First Communion _____

_____

Confirmation _____

_____

In the space below, draw a symbol for one of the Sacraments of Christian Initiation. Tell about the meaning of your chosen symbol.

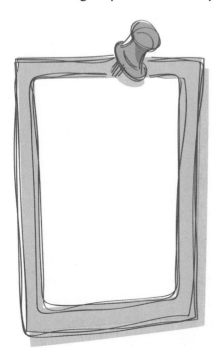

_____

_____

_____

_____

_____

FAITH FACTS

➠ Through Baptism we are born to new life in Christ. We are strengthened by Confirmation, and we are nourished by the Eucharist.

➠ Jesus is truly present in the consecrated bread and wine. Because of this we call the Eucharist the Sacrament of the Real Presence of Jesus.

Words to Know

Sacraments of Christian Initiation
the three sacraments that celebrate membership into the Church: Baptism, Confirmation, and Eucharist

grace
God's free and loving gift to us of his own life and help

Original Sin
the sin of our first parents, Adam and Eve, which led to the sinful condition of all people

Saints and Holy People

Saint John the Baptist (first century)

Saint John the Baptist is Jesus' cousin. You may remember reading about the Virgin Mary's visit to her cousin Elizabeth, who was expecting a child. That child was Saint John the Baptist. As you might also remember, when Mary arrived the child leaped with joy inside his mother's womb. This was because of Jesus' presence, in Mary's womb.

Saint John the Baptist knew in a special way that Jesus was the Savior. For a long time he lived a life of prayer and sacrifice in the desert. He then began to preach about the Kingdom of God. He told people to ask for forgiveness and to be baptized to prepare for the coming of Jesus. Many people went to him to be baptized—even Jesus, who was without sin. John said to Jesus, "I need to be baptized by you, yet you are coming to me?" (Matthew 3:14)

John the Baptist was fearless in telling people not to sin. When he criticized King Herod's sinful behavior, the king had him put in prison. Eventually the king had him killed.

The Church celebrates the feast of John the Baptist on June 24.

Catholic Customs   Sacramentals

When we pray and celebrate the sacraments, we can use certain actions or objects to help us focus our attention on God. These are called sacramentals. Sacramentals help make us holy and prepare us to receive the sacraments. They include blessings, holy water, candles (like the paschal candle on the left), and religious medals or statues, and actions like the Sign of the Cross. Blessings are a very special sacramental. A common blessing you probably know is the blessing of meals. We usually address blessings to the Trinity, by praying the Sign of the Cross.

Make It Happen

Saint John the Baptist told people to get ready for Jesus. He said, "Prepare the way of the Lord, make straight his paths" (Matthew 3:3).

Imagine that you have the job of telling other children your age to get ready for Jesus. What would you tell them? Make a sign that will help children your age be ready for Jesus.

Faith at Home

Celebrating the Sacrament of Baptism is a joyful occasion. Baptism makes us members of God's family, the Church. Talk with your family about each family member's baptism and how the family marked the special day. If someone has not been baptized yet, talk about the reasons why and when he or she will be.

We Pray
Come Holy Ghost

Come, Holy Ghost, Creator blest,
and in our hearts take up thy rest.
Come with thy grace and heavenly
    aid
to fill the hearts which thou hast
    made.
Amen.

Lesson 9 Review

A **Complete** the following sentences, using words from the box.

1. _____ told people to prepare for Jesus' coming.

2. _____ is God's free and loving gift to humans of his own life and help.

3. The first sacrament that unites us to Christ is

   _____ .

4. We become members of the Church through the

   Sacraments of Christian _____ .

5. _____ is the sacrament that anoints us with the Holy Spirit.

Confirmation
Grace
Initiation
John the Baptist
Baptism

B **Fill in** the circle beside the correct answer.

6. When we receive the Eucharist we are forgiven of _____ .
   - ○ venial sin
   - ○ mortal sin
   - ○ Original Sin

7. _____ is another name for the Eucharist.
   - ○ Holy Communion
   - ○ Tabernacle
   - ○ Sacramental

8. The Eucharist is also called the Sacrament of the Real _____.
   - ○ Jesus
   - ○ Presence
   - ○ Communion

9. The sin of our first parents, Adam and Eve, which led to the sinful condition of the human race is called _____ .
   - ○ venial sin
   - ○ mortal sin
   - ○ Original Sin

10. _____ help make us holy and prepare us to receive the sacraments.
    - ○ Sacrifices
    - ○ Sacramentals
    - ○ People

Sacraments of Healing

Let Us Pray

A Prayer for Mercy

All: A clean heart create for me, God; renew within me a steadfast spirit.

Side 1: When I do not show love to others…

All: A clean heart create for me, God; renew within me a steadfast spirit.

Side 2: When I am not truthful…

All: A clean heart create for me, God; renew within me a steadfast spirit.

Side 1: When I do not forgive…

All: A clean heart create for me, God; renew within me a steadfast spirit.

Side 2: When I hurt and feel sad…

All: A clean heart create for me, God; renew within me a steadfast spirit.

Leader: Lord, hear our prayer and show us your love and mercy.

All: Amen.

— Response: Psalm 51:10

My Catholic Faith

God always loves us and cares for us.

➡ **How does knowing this help you when you feel sad?**

Sacred Scripture

God is our loving Father. Like a loving father, God always loves and cares for us. Choosing to **sin** hurts our relationship with God, but he will always show us **mercy**, or kindness, when we ask for forgiveness. Jesus helped his disciples understand this by telling them a parable about a lost son.

More Scripture on Healing and Forgiveness

You can read more about healing and forgiveness in your Bible. Here are some passages:

➠ The Blind Bartimaeus — Mark 10:46–52

➠ The Healing of a Paralytic — Mark 2:1–12

➠ Jairus's Daughter — Luke 8:40–42, 49–56

The Parable of the Prodigal Son

Jesus told a story about a man with two sons. One day the younger son said to his father, "Give me my share of your fortune." The father did so. After a few days the son took all his belongings and set off to a distant country. He wasted all his money and was soon starving. He thought about the workers at his father's farm. They had enough to eat, but he did not.

The son decided to go home to his father and ask for forgiveness. When his father saw him, he was filled with joy. He asked his servants to prepare a feast.

When the older son heard about this, he complained. He said his brother had hurt their father, and did not deserve such a welcome. But the father, who loved his sons equally, replied, "My son, you are here with me always; everything I have is yours. But now we must celebrate and rejoice, because your brother was dead and has come to life again; he was lost and has been found."

— Based on Luke 15:11–32

Living the Scripture

Jesus told the Parable of the Prodigal Son to teach about God's mercy and love.
What does the parable teach you about turning to God when you have sinned?

_____

_____

_____

_____

_____

_____

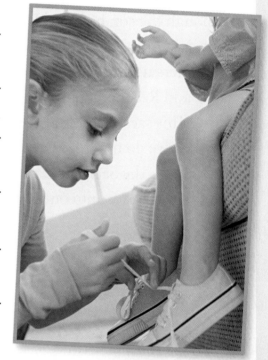

What does it teach you about how to treat others
when they have done something wrong?

_____

_____

_____

_____

_____

_____

_____

Our Catholic Tradition

God Forgives Us and Heals Us

In the Parable of the Prodigal Son, the father forgave his son even though the son had hurt him. He welcomed the son home joyfully. Just like that father, God is always ready to forgive us.

God offers us forgiveness through the Sacrament of Penance and Reconciliation. This is one of the **Sacraments of Healing**. This sacrament is also called Confession. There are times when we do not follow our **conscience** and we make sinful choices. The Sacrament of Penance heals our soul and lets God's grace back into our lives. It is our responsibility to

learn God's law and the Church's teaching. When we do this, our conscience will help us avoid sin.

Sin is anything we say or do that goes against God's law. There are two kinds of sin: mortal sin and venial sin. A **mortal sin** is a serious sin. We commit a mortal sin when we know that something is very wrong but choose to do it anyway. This separates us from God's grace, and makes it harder to make good choices in the future. A **venial sin** does not separate us from God's grace. Still, venial sin hurts our relationship with God. It can also lead us to more serious sin.

God also gives his grace to those who are sick or dying, through the Sacrament of Anointing of the Sick. Celebrating the Sacrament of Anointing of the Sick helps people who are suffering. They are strengthened by God's healing love. They are also reminded that Jesus understands their suffering because he too suffered. This sacrament also grants forgiveness of sin if the person is not able to go to confession.

> What happens in the Sacrament of Penance?

> What's the difference between mortal sin and venial sin?

> How does God help those who are sick?

Live Your Faith

When you listen to your conscience, you do what pleases God. You also avoid what hurts your friendship with him.

List two ways you can do what pleases God at home. Then list two ways you can do what pleases God at school. Choose one item from the list and write about a time you have done this.

At home

1. _____

2. _____

At school

1. _____

2. _____

A time I have put one of these into action

_____

_____

_____

Words to Know

Sacraments of Healing
Penance and the Anointing of the Sick. In these sacraments, God heals our mind, body, and spirit.

conscience
the God-given ability that helps us know right from wrong

mortal sin
a serious sin that separates us from God and his grace

venial sin
a less serious sin against God's law that weakens our relationship with him

Saints and Holy People

Saint John Vianney (1786–1859)

From a young age, John Vianney knew he wanted to become a priest. But because he had little education, he struggled with the lessons in the seminary. Finally, after a great deal of effort and struggle, he was ordained a priest.

Not long after he became a priest, he was sent to a parish in a small French village called Ars. He was sad to discover that many of the people in the village did not care about their faith. But soon, Father John Vianney's reputation as a confessor began to draw people back to church and to the sacraments. He knew just what to say to people who confessed their sins. He helped them know of God's mercy and love for them. His reputation spread, and within a few years thousands of people would come to Ars just to go to confession. Father John often spent sixteen hours a day hearing confessions and counseling people on how to be closer to God. He performed many acts of charity and made great sacrifices for the good of the Kingdom of God.

Saint John Vianney is the patron saint of parish priests. We celebrate his feast day on August 4.

Catholic Customs **Ashes on Ash Wednesday**

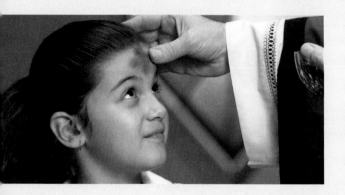

During the Ash Wednesday liturgy, our foreheads are marked with ashes. The ashes remind us of our mortality—that is, that our life on earth will end at our death. They also remind us of our sins. They help us remember that because of Christ's death and Resurrection, we can live forever with God.

Make It Happen

Unscramble each of the words about the Sacrament of Reconciliation and Saint John Vianney. Unscramble the letters that appear in the circles to form another name for the Sacrament of Reconciliation.

IGLEHNA

SOCNOIFENS

CERYM

PEITRS

VESNEROSFIG

Another name for the Sacrament of Reconciliation:

Reach Out!

The Sacrament of Anointing of the Sick brings comfort to those who are sick or suffering. We can also bring comfort to those who are sick by showing love and care.

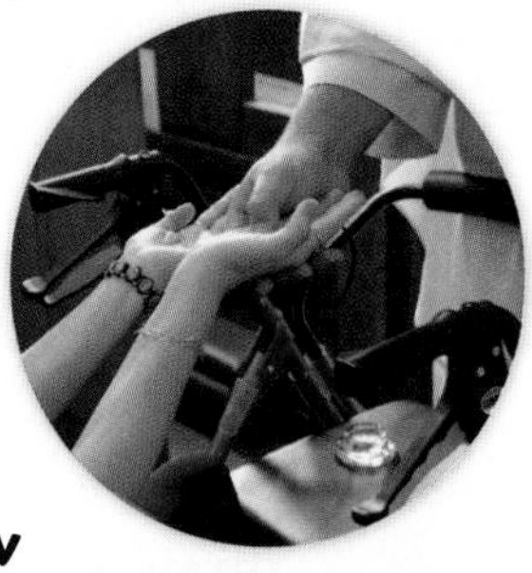

▸ **Think about someone you know who is sick and needs comfort. Be sure to do at least one thing for that person to show love and care.**

We Pray

Act of Hope

O my God,
relying on your infinite goodness
and promises,
I hope to obtain pardon of my sins,
the help of your grace,
and life everlasting,
through the merits of Jesus Christ,
my Lord and Redeemer. Amen.

A **Match** each term in column B with its definition in column A by writing the correct letter in the space provided.

Column A   **Column B**

1. _____ the God-given ability that helps us judge   **a.** conscience
whether actions are right or wrong

2. _____ a serious sin against God's law that separates   **b.** Sacrament
us from God and his grace   of Penance

3. _____ a less serious sin against God's law that   **c.** Sacrament of
weakens our relationship with him   Anointing of the Sick

4. _____ the sacrament that gives us God's forgiveness   **d.** mortal sin
when we have sinned

5. _____ the sacrament that gives God's grace to those   **e.** venial sin
who are suffering in mind, body, or spirit

B **Complete** the following sentences.

6. The Sacraments of Penance and Anointing of the Sick are Sacraments of

_____ .

7. When we learn God's laws, our _____ can help us
make good decisions.

8. Saint John Vianney brought many people back to God through the Sacrament

of _____ .

9. A deliberate thought, word, deed, or omission that goes against God's law is

called a _____ .

10. God has _____ on us, or shows us kindness,
when we ask for forgiveness.

Sacraments at the Service of Communion

Let Us Pray

A Prayer of Blessing

Leader: Lord, thank you for bishops, priests, deacons, and married people.

Reader 1: For bishops who guide us,

All: Lord, grant them your blessing.

Reader 2: For priests, who lead us to you,

All: Lord, grant them your blessing.

Reader 3: For deacons, who teach us,

All: Lord, grant them your blessing.

Reader 4: For married couples, who lead each other to you,

All: Lord, grant them your blessing.

Reader 5: For parents, who show us how to love you,

All: Lord, grant them your blessing.

My Catholic Faith

Think about a married person or a priest that you know.

➡ **How does this person show you how to live as God wants?**

Sacred Scripture

Jesus performed many **miracles** during his time on earth. You might remember some of these. Jesus' first public miracle was at a wedding. Jesus helped the bride and groom by changing water into wine, so that their wedding celebration would not be ruined. This miracle was the beginning of Jesus' public **ministry**.

The Wedding at Cana

On the third day there was a wedding in Cana in Galilee, and the mother of Jesus was there. Jesus and his disciples were also invited to the wedding. When the wine ran short, the mother of Jesus said to him, "They have no wine."

His mother said to the servers, "Do whatever he tells you." Now there were six stone water jars there for Jewish ceremonial washings, each holding twenty to thirty gallons. Jesus told them, "Fill the jars with water." So they filled them to the brim. Then he told them, "Draw some out now and take it to the headwaiter." So they took it. And when the headwaiter tasted the water that had become wine, without knowing where it came from ... the headwaiter called the bridegroom and said to him, "Everyone serves good wine first ... but you have kept the good wine until now." Jesus did this as the beginning of his signs in Cana in Galilee and so revealed his glory, and his disciples began to believe in him.

—John 2:1–3, 5–11

Scripture at Mass

Couples getting married often choose the Scripture about the Wedding Feast at Cana for the Gospel reading at their wedding Mass or ceremony. Another reading that couples often choose is from Saint Paul's First Letter to the Corinthians. That Scripture is about the qualities of love, such as that it is kind, patient, and forgiving (see 1 Corinthians 13).

Living the Scripture

Why do you think Mary told the servers to do whatever Jesus tells them?

_____

_____

_____

Jesus helped the bride and groom by turning water into wine. What are some ways Jesus helps married couples today?

_____

_____

_____

Write a short prayer asking Jesus to help or bless a married couple you know.

_____

_____

_____

Words to Know

miracle
an amazing or wonderful event that happens by the power of God

ministry
a way of being a sign of the Kingdom of God by caring for and serving others

Serving God by Serving Others

As Catholics, we are all called to serve the Church. You do this now by taking care of God's creation and helping your family at home. The Church celebrates two sacraments that especially help us answer this call as adults. These are the Sacrament of Matrimony and the Sacrament of Holy Orders. They are called **Sacraments at the Service of Communion**.

In Holy Orders, baptized men are ordained to serve the Church as bishops, priests, or deacons. Holy Orders imprints

a permanent character on the soul of those who receive it. Bishops promise to use their authority to lead the Church with other bishops and with the Pope. Bishops, priests, and deacons teach us the Gospel message and what it means for our lives. Bishops and priests also lead us in celebrating the sacraments. Without these ordained ministers, the Church would not be complete. But the work of the Church is also done by **lay people**.

One way lay people help God's Church is through the Sacrament of Matrimony, or Marriage. In Marriage, a baptized man and baptized woman promise to be faithful to each other throughout their lives. They commit to sharing married love only with each other. The man and woman also promise to always be open to God's gift of children. They commit to love, care for, and educate any children God gives them. Marriage is celebrated publicly before a priest or deacon, witnesses, and the gathered assembly.

Which sacraments help us to serve the Church as adults?

Who can receive Holy Orders?

What is the Sacrament of Matrimony?

Live Your Faith

Think about a married person or a priest or deacon you know whom you admire. Write about this person. Tell why you admire him or her. Also tell what the person's words or actions teach you.

_____

_____

_____

_____

_____

_____

_____

Words to Know

Sacraments at the Service of Communion
the two sacraments that celebrate people's commitment to serve God and the community: Holy Orders and Matrimony

lay people
all of the baptized people in the Church who share in God's mission but are not ordained; sometimes called the laity

Saints and Holy People

Saint Joseph (first century)

Saint Joseph was Mary's husband and the foster father of Jesus on earth. Before Jesus' birth, an angel came to Joseph in a dream and told him, "Do not be afraid to take Mary your wife into your home. For it is through the holy Spirit that this child has been conceived in her" (Matthew 1:20). Even though Joseph did not understand how this could be, he obeyed God's will. He married Mary and cared for her and Jesus.

When Jesus was a baby, Joseph took him and Mary to Egypt to protect them from King Herod, who wanted to kill all newborn boys. With Mary, Joseph took Jesus to the Temple to present him to God. When Jesus was lost in the Temple at age twelve, Joseph helped Mary find him.

Joseph was a carpenter, and he taught Jesus how to be a carpenter, too. We don't know how Saint Joseph died, but we believe Mary and Jesus were with him. Today, we pray to Saint Joseph for a happy and peaceful death.

The Church honors Saint Joseph on March 19 and on the Feast of the Holy Family, on the Sunday after Christmas.

Catholic Customs — The Domestic Church

Did you know that a Catholic family is known as the "domestic church"? That's because the family is the "school of holiness." It's where we learn who God is and how to live a Christian life. It is also the first place where we learn what it means to live in a community. The family is where we learn to love others.

Make It Happen

Find the following words in the word search below. Then write a sentence about Saint Joseph using at least two of these words.

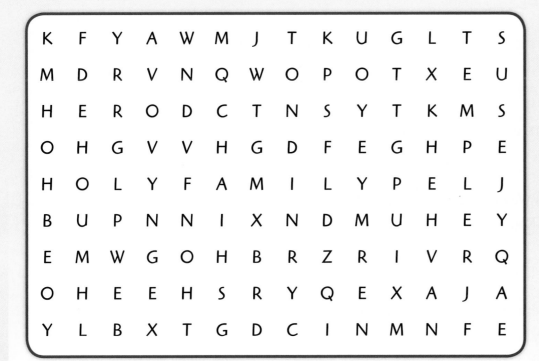

K	F	Y	A	W	M	J	T	K	U	G	L	T	S
M	D	R	V	N	Q	W	O	P	O	T	X	E	U
H	E	R	O	D	C	T	N	S	Y	T	K	M	S
O	H	G	V	V	H	G	D	F	E	G	H	P	E
H	O	L	Y	F	A	M	I	L	Y	P	E	L	J
B	U	P	N	N	I	X	N	D	M	U	H	E	Y
E	M	W	G	O	H	B	R	Z	R	I	V	R	Q
O	H	E	E	H	S	R	Y	Q	E	X	A	J	A
Y	L	B	X	T	G	D	C	I	N	M	N	F	E

Mary

Joseph

angel

Temple

Holy Family

Herod

Egypt

Jesus

Faith at Home

Every day this week, pray for a married couple that is important to your family (such as your parents or grandparents), a priest you know (such as the pastor at your parish), or  someone who teaches you about your faith. Invite family members to take turns naming people to pray for.

We Pray
A Marriage Prayer

Loving Father,
we ask you to hear our prayers and to bless all those united in Matrimony, that we may always know of your mercy and love for us. We ask this through Jesus Christ, our Lord. Amen.
—Based on the *Rite of Marriage*

Lesson 11 Review

A **Complete** each sentence with the letter of the correct word or words from the box.

1. The family is the place where we learn who God is and how to live a Christian life. Because of this, the family is called the ____.

2. The visible sign of the Sacrament of Holy Orders is the ____.

3. The visible sign of the Sacrament of Matrimony is the ____.

4. A ____ is an amazing or wonderful event that happens by the power of God

5. A ____ is a way of caring for and serving others and being a sign of the Kingdom of God.

> **a.** ministry
>
> **b.** exchange of vows
>
> **c.** domestic church
>
> **d.** miracle
>
> **e.** Laying on of Hands

B **Fill in** the circle beside the correct answer.

6. The two sacraments that celebrate people's commitment to serve God and the community are ____ .

   ○ the Sacraments of Healing   ○ the Sacraments at the Service of Communion   ○ Holy Orders and Eucharist

7. Baptized men are ordained as bishops, priests, or deacons in the Sacrament of ____ .

   ○ Eucharist   ○ Holy Orders   ○ Matrimony

8. All of the baptized people in the Church who share in God's mission but are not ordained are called ____ .

   ○ lay people   ○ deacons   ○ married couples

9. In the Sacrament of ____ a baptized man and a baptized woman make a lifelong commitment to love each other and care for their children.

   ○ Eucharist   ○ Holy Orders   ○ Matrimony

10. Before Jesus' birth, ____ came to Joseph in a dream to tell him to marry Mary.

   ○ Jesus   ○ an angel   ○ King Herod

BEING CATHOLIC

Dying and Rising with Jesus

Life is a mixture of happy and sad times, suffering and joy, beauty and destruction. Some bad things in life are caused by forces of nature. For example, hurricanes, tornadoes, and floods destroy property and cause death. Some bad things happen because of illness. And some bad things happen because of accidents. Innocent people suffer as a result.

Sometimes people suffer because of the evil other people choose to do. A kid is bullied at school, an elderly man is robbed and hurt, a fight breaks out because of jealousy or anger. Worse, sometimes people are killed because of hatred and violence.

Suffering like this is caused by the selfish choices people sometimes make. Even though God created us for a life of goodness and love, Original Sin means we are sometimes weak and cannot resist temptation and sin. In turn, our sins can bring hurt and suffering to others.

Thinking about Suffering

Tell about someone you know who suffered because of an accident, illness, or a natural disaster.

_____

How did that make you feel? _____

_____

Describe a time when someone you know or heard about suffered because of the selfish actions of another person.

_____

What do you think can make a person act selfishly? _____

_____

We Share in New Life with Jesus

The fact that God permits physical and even moral evil in our world is a mystery we can't understand. But because of Jesus we can always have hope. Jesus' love gives us strength, and his mercy gives us comfort. Especially because of Jesus' death on the Cross and his Resurrection, we have hope that joy can follow pain and sadness.

Jesus died for our sins. He restored our friendship with God. He also healed the sin that causes hurt and destruction.

Jesus also rose again, and then ascended to Heaven. Because of Jesus' suffering, death, Resurrection, and Ascension, we know that we can also experience joy after suffering. We also know that after death, we can know the greatest joy of all: the joy of being united with the Blessed Trinity in Heaven. We begin our journey toward this union at our Baptism.

Hope in the Resurrection

Name a time when you were worried or hurt. What did you hope for?

_____

How can Jesus' Resurrection give you hope in hard times?

_____

_____

Think about what it means to have hope. Write a prayer of hope.

Dear God, _____

_____

_____

Life in Christ

The Word of God is a light for our path. We must assimilate it in faith and prayer and put it into practice. (*CCC*, 1802)

The Ten Commandments

1. I am the LORD your God. You shall not have other gods besides me.

2. You shall not take the name of the LORD, your God, in vain.

3. Remember to keep holy the Sabbath day.

4. Honor your father and mother.

5. You shall not kill.

6. You shall not commit adultery.

7. You shall not steal.

8. You shall not bear false witness against your neighbor.

9. You shall not covet your neighbor's wife.

10. You shall not covet anything that belongs to your neighbor.

God Created Us in His Image

Let Us Pray

A Prayer of Thanks and Praise

Leader: Loving God, help us appreciate the marvelous gifts of the world you have created.

Reader: Lord, you have given everything its place in the world, and no one can make it otherwise. For it is your creation, the heavens and the earth and the stars: you are Lord of all.
— From the *Roman Missal* (cf. Est 4:17)

All: We praise you, Lord, for all the wonders of creation. We thank you for the goodness of all you have created. Help us to love and care for all creation. Amen.

My Catholic Faith
God created a wonderful world. He also created a wonderful you!
➠ **What can you do today to say thank you to God for his creation?**

Sacred Scripture

Have you ever looked up at the night sky to count the stars? Have you ever seen a beautiful flower about to bloom, or a newborn baby, so perfectly formed? Have you felt wonder at where all these marvelous things in our world come from?

In the first book of the Bible, the Book of Genesis, we learn about the story of **creation**.

God Creates Us and All the World

In the beginning, when there was nothing, God created the heavens and the earth. He created light. He then separated light from darkness and made night and day. He created the sky and the oceans, and the dry land of the earth. God created every kind of plant and tree that bears fruit. He created the stars and sun and moon. He created all the fish of the seas and the birds of the sky, and animals to fill the land.

God then said, "I will make people in my own image. I will give them authority over the fish of the sea, the birds of the air, and over all the creatures of the earth."

God created man and woman. He blessed them and said to them, "Be fruitful and multiply. Have power over the fish of the sea, the birds of the air, and the living things on earth."

And so it was. God looked at everything he had made, and he found it very good.

—Based on Genesis 1:1–31

More Scripture on Creation

You can read about creation in other Scripture passages. Here are some:

➠ God Created the Heavens and Stars — Job 9:5–9

➠ From the Earth We Were Formed — Proverbs 8:23–29

➠ In God We Have Our Being — Acts 17:24–28

Living the Scripture

Draw a picture that tells part of the story of creation. Give your picture a title. At the bottom of your picture, write a quote from the Scripture account of creation that helps explain the picture.

_____

_____

_____

Our Catholic Tradition

God Made Us Special

The story of creation in the Bible tells us about all the wonderful things God created. It also tells us how special we are to God.

Of all the living things he created, God made us special by creating us in his own image. Like Jesus, his own Son made man, we are the image of the invisible God. God made us

spiritual beings with a body and a soul. Our soul comes from God. It is part of us from the moment we come into being, before we are born. God also made us to have a natural desire to know him and to love him. Even though the Bible does not tell us scientific facts about creation, it tells us that God is the Creator. He created the universe and all people. He created the universe out of love for us.

The story of creation also tells us that God created humans to live in community. He calls all people to love and care for one another. God created Adam and Eve, the first man and first woman, for each other. This bond between man and woman has always been the first way people form a community. Like Adam and Eve, God created men and women for each other.

God calls all people to care for his creation. We respond through **stewardship**. Being stewards of creation means we have a responsibility to protect and care for all that God has created. We must also use creation for the good of all people.

> How did God make us special?

> Who were the first man and woman?

> What is our responsibility for God's creation?

Live Your Faith

We are called to care for God's creation. For each of the items in the chart, write a way people sometimes do not take care of creation. Then write or draw at least one way you can be a good steward of creation.

	Ways of Not Caring	Ways to Care
My family		
Those who are sick or poor		
The environment		
Plants and animals		

Words to Know

stewardship
caring for and protecting the gifts of creation that God has given us

Saints and Holy People

Saint Marianne Cope (1838–1918)

Marianne Cope was raised in a small town in Upstate New York. When she was old enough to work, she took a job in a factory so that she could help support her family. She later became a religious sister.

Sister Marianne served as a teacher, and then as superior of her religious order. Then she was asked to be the superior of a Catholic hospital. At the hospital, she learned a great deal about caring for sick and suffering people.

When the king and queen of Hawaii asked for volunteers to help them run a hospital, Mother Marianne went and took a group of sisters with her. In Hawaii, Sister Marianne tended to the care of lepers, people with a contagious skin disease. She transformed dirty hospitals into beautiful places where lepers can get good care. She opened homes and other facilities to help them and their families.

Mother Marianne Cope dedicated her life to the care of lepers, who were often shunned by society.

Mother Marianne Cope was canonized, or named a saint, by Pope Benedict XVI in 2012. Her feast day is January 23.

Catholic Customs   Stained Glass Windows

How many times have you seen stained glass windows in church? How often have you looked closely at the images in those windows? Stained glass windows have been used in churches for more than a thousand years. A long time ago, before most people were able to read, stained glass windows were a way to teach people about God. The windows may have shown images of Jesus, of the Virgin Mary or saints, or of scenes from Scripture, such as the story of creation. The next time you are in church, be sure to take a close look at the images in the stained glass windows.

Make It Happen

Saint Marianne Cope took care of sick people whom society rejected. She understood that all people are made in God's image. What can you learn from Saint Marianne Cope's example? Write a story about a time you cared for someone in need. Tell how your actions showed love.

_____

_____

_____

_____

_____

Reach Out!

When God created the world, he gave us the job of caring for creation. How can you do your share?

➠ **Name two things you will do this week to care for creation.**

We Pray

A Prayer of Praise

O LORD, our Lord,
  how awesome is your name
    through all the earth!
When I see your heavens, the work
  of your fingers,
the moon and stars that you set in
    place—
All sheep and oxen,
  even the beasts of the fields,
The birds of the air, the fish of the
    sea.
O LORD, our Lord,
  how awesome is your name
    through all the earth!
                          —Psalm 8:2, 4, 8–9

Lesson 12 Review

A **Complete** the following sentences, using words from the box. Two words are used twice.

1. _____ is caring for and protecting the gifts of creation that God has given us.

2. Saint Marianne Cope cared for people who were shunned by society. She understood that all people are created in the _____ of God.

3. We must use God's _____ for the good of all people.

4. God gave men and women equal _____ . He created them for each other and to share the gift of children.

Genesis
stewardship
soul
dignity
community
image
love
creation

5. _____ is everything in the world made by God.

6. God created the universe out of _____ for us.

7. God created humans to live in _____ .

8. In the Bible, we can read the story of creation in the Book of _____ .

9. God made us special by creating us in his own _____ .

10. Our _____ comes from God. It is part of us from the moment we come into being, before we are born.

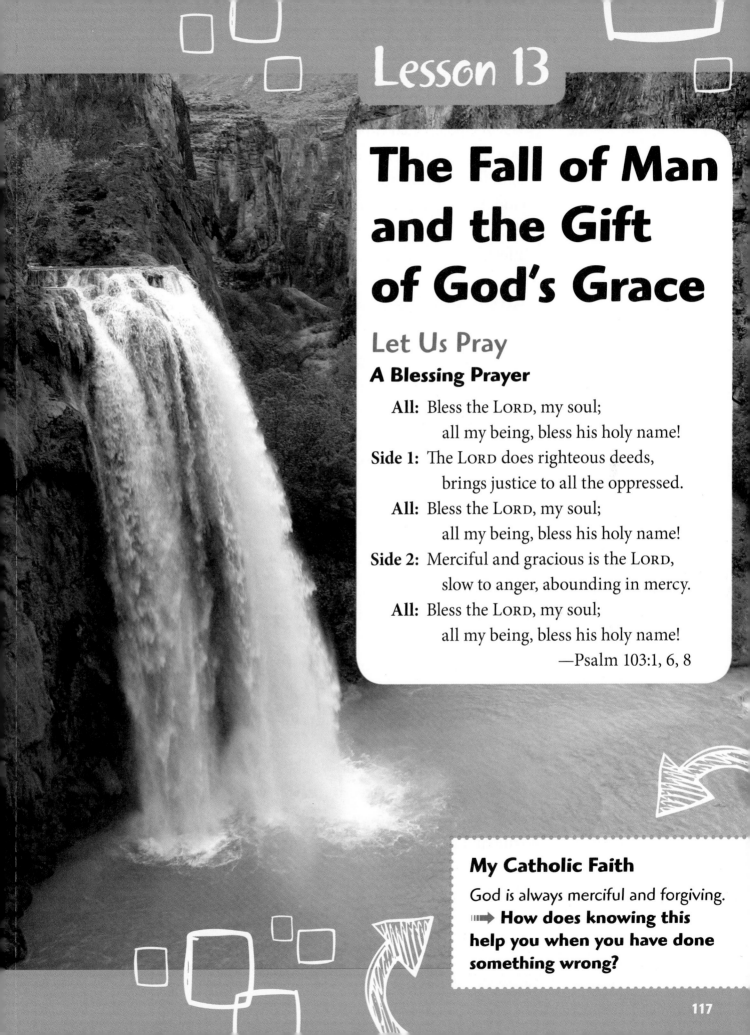

The Fall of Man and the Gift of God's Grace

Let Us Pray

A Blessing Prayer

All: Bless the LORD, my soul;
    all my being, bless his holy name!

Side 1: The LORD does righteous deeds,
    brings justice to all the oppressed.

All: Bless the LORD, my soul;
    all my being, bless his holy name!

Side 2: Merciful and gracious is the LORD,
    slow to anger, abounding in mercy.

All: Bless the LORD, my soul;
    all my being, bless his holy name!

—Psalm 103:1, 6, 8

My Catholic Faith

God is always merciful and forgiving.
➡ **How does knowing this help you when you have done something wrong?**

Sacred Scripture

When God created Adam and Eve, the first man and first woman, they lived in perfect happiness. But then they gave in to **temptation**, and they used their **free will** to disobey God. When they did this, Adam and Eve committed the first sin. They lost the perfect holiness God had given them. This affected them and all human beings.

Adam and Eve Disobey God

The LORD God created Adam and Eve. They lived in the Garden of Eden. God had filled the garden with trees that were beautiful to look at and good for food. In the middle of the garden God set the tree of the knowledge of good and evil. God told Adam and Eve they could eat the fruit of any tree except the tree of knowledge.

A serpent lived in the garden. The serpent asked Eve, "Did God really tell you not to eat from the tree of knowledge?" Eve answered: "God said, 'You shall not eat it or even touch it, or you will die.'" But the serpent said to her: "You certainly will not die if you eat of that tree! No, God knows that the moment you eat its fruit your eyes will be opened and you will become wise. You will be like gods."

Eve looked at the tree and saw that it was good for food. She also wanted the wisdom it gave. So she took some of its fruit and ate it. She also gave some to Adam, who was with her, and he ate it. Then their eyes were opened, and they realized that they were naked. They sewed fig leaves together and made loincloths for themselves. When God saw that Adam and Eve had disobeyed him, he sent them out of the Garden of Eden.

—Based on Genesis 2:7–9; 3:1–7

Scripture at Mass

The Scripture passage about Adam and Eve disobeying God is read at Mass during Lent. This is a good Scripture reading for Lent. It reminds us that Adam and Eve's sin hurt our relationship with God, and that Jesus healed our relationship with God.

Living the Scripture

Write a story about temptation based on the story of Adam and Eve. But in your story, let the characters make a good choice and have a good ending.

1. **Adam and Even are in the Garden of Eden.**
   Who are the characters in your story? What is the setting?

   _____

   _____

2. **Adam and Eve give in to the temptation. They eat the fruit God told them not to eat.** Unlike Adam and Eve, your characters resist temptation. What do they think or say as they turn away from temptation?

   _____

   _____

   _____

3. **Adam and Eve have to leave the Garden of Eden. They lose the happiness they had with God.** What happens for your characters? How do they feel?

   _____

   _____

   _____

   _____

Words to Know

temptation
wanting to do something we should not or not do something we should

free will
our God-given freedom and ability to make choices

Our Catholic Tradition

God Helps Us Live Holy Lives

All people find it hard to turn away from temptation sometimes. The story of Adam and Eve in the Garden of Eden can help us understand why. When Adam and Eve disobeyed God, their sin did not affect only them. It affected all people. Because of their sin, we are weak and sometimes disobey God. Adam and Eve's sin took away our original holiness. Their sin and the way it affects all people is called Original Sin. Because of Original Sin, we sometimes have trouble staying away from temptation and sin.

Also like Adam and Eve, we have freedom to choose whether to obey God and follow his law. If we do not know that something is sinful, our responsibility for that action is reduced. But we are responsible to learn about God's law and his will so that we can make good choices that please him.

God helps us live good and holy lives by giving us **virtues**. There are two kinds of virtues: Cardinal Virtues and Theological Virtues.

Even though we sometimes do not follow God's will, he is always forgiving. We first receive God's mercy, or forgiveness, at our Baptism. Through Baptism, the Holy Spirit gives us grace that takes away our sin and unites us with Jesus. We also receive God's mercy in the Sacrament of Penance. The Holy Spirit, the Third Divine Person of the Trinity, leads us back to God when we sin. This is part of God's gift of grace.

> What is Original Sin?

> How can we learn to make good choices?

> How can we receive God's grace when we sin?

Live Your Faith

Adam and Eve knew God's will, but went against it. What are some ways children your age may be tempted to go against God's will?

_____

_____

How can you become stronger in following your conscience at times like these?

_____

_____

Draw or write about a time when you followed your conscience and didn't give in to temptation.

Words to Know

virtues
good spiritual habits that make us stronger and help us do what is right and good

Saints and Holy People

Saint Michael the Archangel

In the Bible we often read about angels. For example, at the time of Jesus' Resurrection, two angels appeared to the disciples at Jesus' tomb.

Angels are spiritual creatures who glorify God. They are also his messengers and protectors of his people. Angels in the Bible usually do not have a name. But three of the angels in the Bible are named. These three are a special kind of angel called an *archangel*. In the Book of Revelation in the Bible, we read about the archangel Michael defeating the devil in a battle. Because of this, artists often show Saint Michael the Archangel slaying a serpent or a dragon with a sword.

Saint Michael the Archangel is known as the guardian of the Church. He is also a protector of all people in times of danger, and he is the patron saint of police officers. The Church celebrates his feast day on September 29.

The other archangels are Gabriel and Raphael. You might remember that the angel Gabriel came to Mary to tell her that God wanted her to be the Mother of his Son, Jesus. Raphael appears in the Old Testament to guide a man named Tobias on an important journey.

Catholic Customs Pilgrimages

A pilgrimage is a journey to a holy site to pray for a special blessing. People have been going on pilgrimages since the time of Jesus. Today Catholics make pilgrimages to many holy places, such as Rome and the Holy Land. Other popular pilgrimage sites are shrines dedicated to Mary. One of these is Lourdes, in France. About five million pilgrims visit Lourdes every year!

Make It Happen

Find the following words from the story of Saint Michael the Archangel in the word search.

D	R	A	G	O	N	R	A	P	H	A	E	L	G
Y	C	M	E	S	S	E	N	G	E	R	X	E	G
A	H	G	A	B	R	I	E	L	X	R	B	A	M
A	R	C	H	A	N	G	E	L	V	B	A	H	Z
E	S	E	R	P	E	N	T	D	M	C	Z	C	O
N	P	R	O	T	E	C	T	O	R	T	V	I	D
O	K	Y	R	R	J	T	J	X	F	N	D	M	A

archangel

dragon

Gabriel

messenger

Michael

protector

Raphael

serpent

Faith at Home

The *Confiteor*, the prayer to the right, is from the Mass. Learn this prayer with your family and talk about its meaning.

We Pray
The Confiteor

I confess to almighty God
and to you, my brothers and sisters,
that I have greatly sinned,
in my thoughts and in my words,
in what I have done
    and in what I have failed to do,
through my fault, through my fault,
through my most grievous fault;
therefore I ask blessed Mary,
    ever-Virgin,
all the Angels and Saints,
and you, my brothers and sisters,
to pray for me to the Lord our God.
—*Roman Missal*

Lesson 13 Review

A **Complete** each sentence with the letter of the correct word or words from the box.

1. Because of Adam and Eve's sin, all people sometimes find it hard to resist _____ .

2. Adam and Eve's sin took away our _____ .

3. Adam and Eve's sin and the way it affects all people is called _____ .

4. God helps us make good choices and live good and holy lives by giving us _____ .

5. We first receive God's _____ , or forgiveness, at our Baptism.

> a. virtues
>
> b. temptation
>
> c. Original Sin
>
> d. mercy
>
> e. original holiness

B **Fill in** the circle beside the correct answer.

6. _____ is wanting to do something we should not do.
   ○ **Temptation**   ○ **Free will**   ○ **Virtue**

7. God told Adam and Eve not to eat from the _____ .
   ○ **apple tree**   ○ **tree of knowledge**   ○ **fruit trees in the garden**

8. Our God-given freedom and ability to make choices is called _____ .
   ○ **free will**   ○ **temptation**   ○ **virtues**

9. _____ is/are good spiritual habits that make us stronger and help us do what is right and good.
   ○ **Virtues**   ○ **Temptation**   ○ **Free will**

10. The Archangel Michael is known as the protector of _____ .
    ○ **the Church**   ○ **the Scriptures**   ○ **Jesus' tomb**

The Church Is Our Mother and Teacher

Let Us Pray

A Prayer for the Church

Leader: Let us pray for the Church and for all those who teach and guide us.

Reader 1: We pray for the Pope and all the bishops. Guide them always.

All: Lord, please guide your people.

Reader 2: We pray for all priests, deacons, and all religious brothers and sisters. Guide them in teaching us the faith.

All: Lord, please guide your people.

Reader 3: We pray for our families, who teach us to make choices that please you.

All: Lord, please guide your people.

Leader: Lord, please bless us and bless all those who show us the way to live as your disciples.

All: Amen.

My Catholic Faith

The Church is one family of God.
➠ **In what ways is the Church like a family?**

125

Sacred Scripture

Saint Paul the Apostle wrote many letters to the early Christian communities. In these letters, he taught the early Christians what it means to be part of Jesus' Church. The Scripture passage you are about to read is from one of Paul's letters. In the letter, Saint Paul explains that all Christians are members of God's family, the Church.

The Church Is One in Jesus

Grace to you and peace from God our Father. Blessed be God who chose us to be his children.

Remember that at one time, you were without Christ. You were without hope and far from God. But Jesus came and preached peace to everyone, and now you are no longer strangers or wanderers. You are fellow citizens with the saints and members of God's family. The Church is built upon the foundation of the Apostles. And Jesus is the center stone that holds it all together. Because of Jesus, together you are a single dwelling place of the Holy Spirit.

—Based on Ephesians 1:2–5;
2:11–13, 19–22

More Scripture on the Church

➠ The Communal Life of the Early Church — Acts 2:42–47

➠ The Growth of the Early Church — Acts 5:12–16

➠ The Church as the Body of Christ — Ephesians 1:15–23

Living the Scripture

Saint Paul reminds the early Christians what life was like before Jesus came into the world. Think about what life before Jesus may have been like. Tell how the people may have felt at this time.

_____

_____

_____

Saint Paul also reminds the early Christians that Jesus came and brought peace. He tells them that because of Jesus, they are no longer strangers. They are one family of God. Describe some feelings the people may have had after knowing Jesus and his teachings.

_____

_____

_____

Think about a time in your life when you learned something important about Jesus. What did you learn? How did it change you or help you?

_____

_____

_____

_____

Our Catholic Tradition

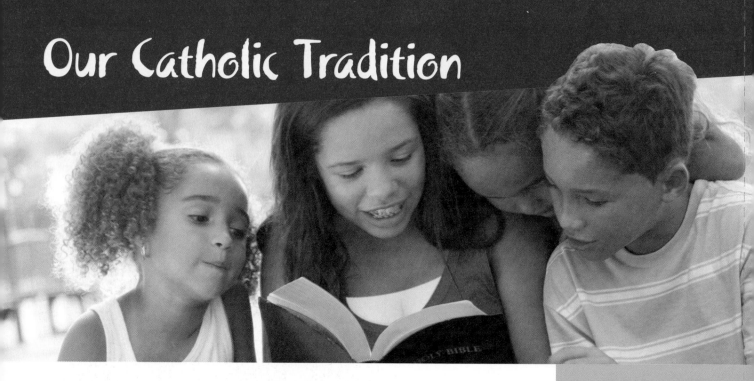

The Church Teaches Us God's Law

Who helps you know the difference between right and wrong? You probably learn a lot from your family. You also learn rules about how to respect yourself and others at school. And you are also guided by your conscience, your God-given ability to know what is good and what is bad. Along with all of this, the Bible and the teachings of the Church also guide you.

The Bible teaches us what it means to live as God's people. In the Old Testament, the Ten Commandments give us a summary of God's law. God's law in the Old Testament is called the Old Law. This does not mean it is old or outdated, but that it is from before Jesus. The Old Law prepares us for the Gospel message of Jesus. In the New Testament we learn the New Law. This is all of Jesus' teachings about how to live as Christians. We can learn a lot about how to live **moral** lives from Jesus' teachings in the Sermon on the Mount. Jesus taught us that the foundation to a moral life is love—love for God and for others.

The Church helps us understand everything in the Bible and what it tells us about how to live. Through the Church's Magisterium, we learn God's law and how to follow it in our daily lives. By following the Magisterium's teachings, we can live in eternal happiness with God.

How do we know right from wrong?

What is the foundation for a moral life?

How does the Church help us know how to live?

Live Your Faith

In the Church, we are all one family of God. The Church is like a parent to all the members of this family. She teaches us about God and how to live as Christians.

In the space below, list people who teach you to live your Christian faith. First, list people in the Church, then people in your family, then other people.

Who teaches me to live as a Christian?

In the Church

_____

_____

_____

In my family

_____

_____

_____

Others

_____

_____

_____

FAITH FACTS

➡ The Church, as the **Communion of Saints**, seeks the salvation of all people. The Church entrusts those who have died to God's mercy. She prays for their eternal reward in Heaven.

➡ We can find some basic rules about how to live as Christians in the Precepts of the Church.

➡ Celebrating the liturgy and the sacraments are more ways the Church helps us to live a moral life.

Words to Know

moral
in right relationship with God, yourself, and others

Communion of Saints
everyone who believes in and follows Jesus—people on earth and people who have died and are in Purgatory or Heaven

Saints and Holy People

Saint Paul (first century)

Saint Paul was one of the great saints of the early Church. He brought the Good News to countless people and helped the Church grow.

Unlike Saint Peter or the other Apostles, Saint Paul was not a follower of Jesus during Jesus' time on earth. In fact, at first Saint Paul was an enemy of those who believed in Jesus. He wanted to punish and even kill the early Christians. Saint Paul came to believe in Jesus when he had a vision of the Risen Jesus. Paul then became a Christian and a **missionary**.

Saint Paul traveled to cities that had not yet heard about Jesus. With his close followers, he would preach about Jesus. Many people were baptized. In the different cities, believers formed church communities. They began to meet for prayer and to celebrate the Eucharist.

Some of Saint Paul's missionary journeys were to places that were very far away. Some took several years by foot or by boat. Because of Saint Paul's work, the Church spread throughout the Roman Empire.

Saint Paul shares a feast day with Saint Peter on June 29.

 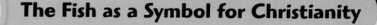

Catholic Customs — The Fish as a Symbol for Christianity

Have you ever seen a fish symbol used to represent Christianity? This symbol has been used since the time of the early Christians, almost two thousand years ago. The symbol represents Jesus, and connects to Jesus' multiplication of the loaves and fishes. It also connects to other Scripture events, such as Jesus calling two fishermen to be the first Apostles.

Make It Happen

Saint Paul traveled to faraway places to teach others about Jesus. You can teach others about Jesus without going far away. In each space below, draw a place where you can teach about Jesus' love.

Words to Know

missionary
a person who answers God's call to help people all over the world know about Jesus

Reach Out!

Because of Saint Paul many people came to know about Jesus and his love.

➡ **How can your friends or classmates know about Jesus' love because of you?**

We Pray

Act of Love

O my God, I love you above all things, with my whole heart and soul, because you are all good and worthy of all love. I love my neighbor as myself for the love of you. I forgive all who have injured me, and ask pardon of all whom I have injured. Amen.

Lesson 14 Review

A Complete the crossword puzzle.

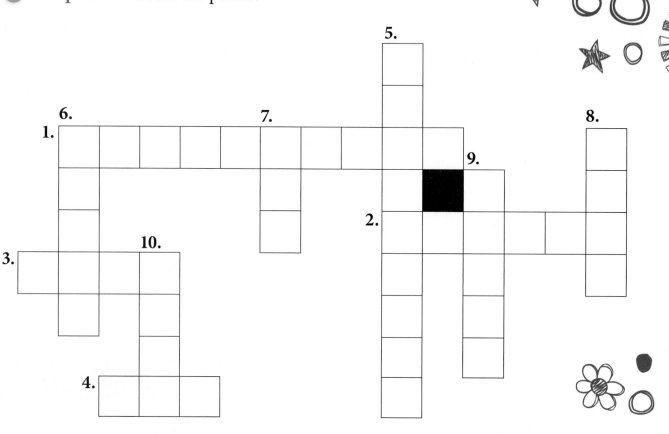

Across

1. A _____ is a person who answers God's call to help people all over the world know about Jesus.

2. The Communion of _____ is everyone who believes in and follows Jesus—people on Earth or in Purgatory or Heaven.

3. Saint _____ wrote many letters to the early Christian communities.

4. The _____ Law is the law of love Jesus taught in the Gospels.

Down

5. Saint Paul met the Risen Jesus and became a _____.

6. To live a _____ life means to be in right relationship with God, yourself, and others.

7. The _____ Law is God's law in the Old Testament, summed up in the Ten Commandments.

8. The early Christians used a _____ symbol to show that they were followers of Jesus.

9. The Church helps us understand everything in the _____ and what it means for our lives.

10. Jesus taught us that the foundation of a moral life is _____.

The Ten Commandments:
Love the Lord, Your God

Let Us Pray

A Prayer of Petition

Leader: We bless you and adore you, Lord.

Group 1: Teach us to put you first in our lives, and to know that all glory is yours.

All: Our help comes from the Lord, who made heaven and earth.

Group 2: Teach us to worship you and to make time to praise and adore you.

All: Our help comes from the Lord, who made heaven and earth.

Group 3: Guide us in following your commandments, and to always act with love for you and for all.

All: Our help comes from the Lord, who made heaven and earth.

Leader: We ask this through Jesus, our Lord.

All: Amen.

(Refrain based on Psalm 121:2)

My Catholic Faith

There are many ways to show love for God in our daily lives.

➡ **What are some ways you show love for God?**

Sacred Scripture

Long ago, before the time of Jesus, God made a covenant, or a sacred promise, with the Israelites. Part of the covenant is the Ten Commandments. The Ten Commandments helped the Israelites know how to keep their promise to God.

The Ten Commandments

The Lord God gave these commandments to Moses on Mount Sinai.

I am the LORD, your God. You shall not have strange gods before me.

You shall not take the name of the LORD, you God, in vain.

Remember to keep holy the LORD's day.

Honor your father and your mother.

You shall not kill.

You shall not commit adultery.

You shall not steal.

You shall not bear false witness against your neighbor.

You shall not covet your neighbor's wife or your neighbor's goods.

—Based on Exodus 19:20; 20:1–17

In the Gospels, Jesus explains God's law of the Old Testament.

The Great Commandment

A man asked Jesus which of the commandments is most important. Jesus answered: "The first is this ... 'You shall love the Lord your God with all your heart, with all your soul, with all your mind, and with all your strength.' The second is this: 'You shall love your neighbor as yourself.' There is no other commandment greater than these."

—Based on Mark 12:28–31

Scripture at Mass

We hear the Scripture about the commandments, from the Book of Exodus, at Mass during Lent. Why do you think this is a good reading for us to hear and think about in Lent?

Living the Scripture

Choose one of the first three commandments from the Scripture reading, and create a banner for the commandment. Along with writing the commandment on the banner, write words and symbols that tell how to live it.

Our Catholic Tradition

The First Three Commandments: Love of God

How well do you know the **Ten Commandments**? You've probably seen images of the stone tablets of the commandments, but do you know each of the commandments? Do you know what each tells you about how to live your life each day?

The first three commandments tell us how to be faithful to God. The other seven tell us how to treat other people with love. In this lesson, you will learn about the first three commandments.

In the Ten Commandments, God gave his law to all people. God's commandments are based on the **natural law**. The natural law is present in every person's heart. It expresses the dignity of all people. The natural law includes the values that all people accept as right. For example, people everywhere understand that no person can kill another unjustly. Everyone must obey the natural law, because everyone is created by God.

What do the Ten Commandments teach us?

What is the natural law?

The Commandment	What the Commandment Means
1 I am the LORD, your God. You shall not have strange gods before me.	• Place your faith in God alone. • Don't make other things in your life more important than God. • Believe in, trust, and love God.
2 You shall not take the name of the LORD, your God, in vain.	• Speak God's name with reverence. • Don't use the name of God, Jesus Christ, Mary, or the saints in a disrespectful way.
3 Remember to keep holy the LORD's Day.	• Gather to celebrate the Eucharist on Sunday and Holy Days of Obligation. • Rest and avoid unnecessary work on Sunday. Spend time with family and serving those in need.

Live Your Faith

In each frame below, draw something you can do to follow the Third Commandment.

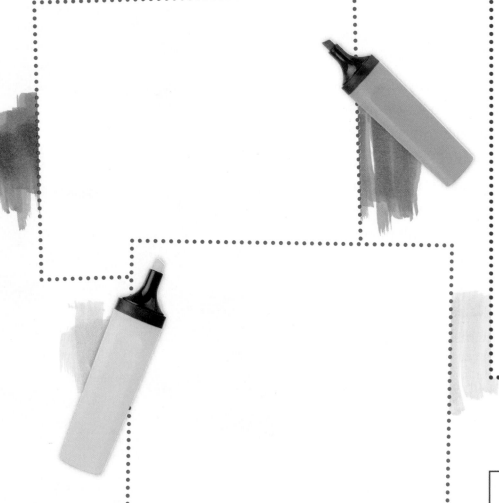

FAITH FACTS

➡ The natural law never changes. It guides all people in all time. It guides the laws for how we live in society.

➡ The Ten Commandments help us understand the natural law and what it means for our lives. They tell us the minimum that is required to love God and others.

➡ God gives us the grace to follow his commandments.

Words to Know

Ten Commandments
the laws that God gave Moses on Mount Sinai. They tell us what is required to love God and others.

natural law
rules about goodness that are written in our hearts and are natural to follow

Saints and Holy People

Saint Teresa Benedicta of the Cross (Edith Stein) (1891–1942)

Edith Stein was raised in a Jewish home, where her parents taught her the Jewish faith. When Edith was a teenager, she turned away from her faith. For many years, she did not pray or even believe in God.

When Edith was a student in college, she read the autobiography of Saint Teresa of Ávila, a saint who lived in the sixteenth century. The story of Saint Teresa and her love for God made a great impression on Edith. She wanted to know more about God.

Edith's spiritual journey led her to celebrate the Sacrament of Baptism. Eventually, she followed Saint Teresa's example and became a Carmelite nun. She took the name Teresa Benedicta of the Cross.

Teresa lived with her religious community in the Netherlands. In 1940, the Nazis invaded and took control of that country. The bishops of the Netherlands had criticized the Nazis. To get revenge, the Nazis arrested all Jews in the country who had become Christian. In August 1942, Teresa Benedicta and her sister Rosa, who had also become Catholic, were put to death in a concentration camp.

Pope Saint John Paul II canonized Teresa Benedicta of the Cross in 1999. Her feast day is August 9.

Catholic Customs

Religious Art

Since the time of the early Church, Christians have shown their faith and their love for God through art. This art takes many forms, such as paintings, icons (like the one shown at left), and statues. We do not pray to the images. Instead, the images help us pray and adore God. They also help us honor holy people, such as Mary and the saints.

Make It Happen

Learning about Saint Teresa of Ávila inspired Saint Teresa Benedicta of the Cross. It made her want to be closer to God. Tell about someone you know who shows great love for God. Then tell what this person's example teaches you.

Someone you know

_____

_____

_____

What this person teaches you

_____

_____

_____

Faith at Home

Learn more about the saints with your family. Choose saints from this book or from another resource and read about them with someone in your family. Talk about surprising things you learn, and about what the saints teach you.

We Pray

A Prayer of Praise

We praise you, O God. We profess you as Lord. Everlasting Father, all the world bows down before you. All the angels sing your praise. The heavens and the earth are filled with your majesty and glory. We proclaim our faith in you. Day by day we praise you, now and forever. In your goodness, Lord, keep us free from sin. Have mercy on us. We place our hope in you. Amen.

—Based on the *Te Deum*

Lesson 15 Review

A Complete the following sentences, using words from the box.

1. The _____ are God's laws that tell us what is required to love God and others.

2. Saint Teresa Benedicta of the Cross was inspired to know about God by the story of _____ .

| Ten Commandments |
| God |
| natural law |
| our neighbor |
| Saint Teresa of Ávila |

3. Rules about goodness that are written in our hearts and are natural to follow are known as the _____ .

4. Jesus said the most important commandment is to love _____ with all our heart, all our soul, all our mind, and all our strength.

5. Jesus said the second most important commandment is to love _____ as we love ourselves.

B Draw a line to match each action with the commandment it follows.

6. Believing in and trusting God

7. Speaking God's name with reverence

8. Attending Mass on Sunday

9. Saying the name of God, Jesus, Mary, and the saints only in respectful ways

10. Spending time with family and helping those in need on Sunday

First Commandment

Second Commandment

Third Commandment

The Ten Commandments:

Love Your Neighbor

Let Us Pray

A Prayer of Blessing

Leader: God gave us the commandments to lead us to salvation.

Reader 1: Lord, by honoring my parents, I will show my love for you.

All: Every day I will bless you, Lord. I will praise your name forever.

Reader 2: Lord, by honoring and protecting all human life, I will show my love for you.

All: Every day I will bless you, Lord. I will praise your name forever.

Reader 3: Lord, by respecting myself and respecting others, I will show my love for you.

All: Every day I will bless you, Lord. I will praise your name forever.

(Refrain based on Psalm 145:2)

My Catholic Faith

Jesus said we should love our neighbor as ourselves.

➡ **Who are some people Jesus says are *your* neighbor?**

Sacred Scripture

Do you remember how Jesus summarized the Ten Commandments? He said we must love God above all else and love our neighbor as ourselves. To explain this, Jesus told a parable about an injured man and the person who saved him.

The Parable of the Good Samaritan

A man asked Jesus, "Who is my neighbor?"
Jesus answered by telling this story.

"A man fell victim to robbers as he went down from Jerusalem to Jericho. They stripped and beat him and went off leaving him half-dead. A priest happened to be going down that road, but when he saw him, he passed by on the opposite side. Likewise a Levite came to the place, and when he saw him, he passed by on the opposite side. But a Samaritan traveler who came upon him was moved with compassion at the sight. He approached the victim, poured oil and wine over his wounds and bandaged them. Then he lifted him up on his own animal, took him to an inn and cared for him."

Jesus then said to the man who asked him the question:

"Which of these three, in your opinion, was neighbor to the robbers' victim?" He answered, "The one who treated him with mercy." Jesus said to him, "Go and do likewise."

—Luke 10:29–34, 36–37

More Scripture on Loving Our Neighbor

➡ The Rich Young Man — Matthew 19:16–22

➡ God Is Love — 1 John 4:20–21

➡ The Golden Rule — Matthew 7:12

Living the Scripture

Have you ever heard someone described as a Good Samaritan? Calling someone a Good Samaritan is a way to say that the person showed kindness. It means the person helped out a stranger in need, like the Samaritan in Jesus' parable.

Do you know someone who was a Good Samaritan? Or have you heard about a Good Samaritan in the news? In the space below, write a news article about this person. Tell how he or she helped a stranger in need. Add a title and a picture to your news story.

THE NEWS

Our Catholic Tradition

Commandments 4 through 10: Love of Neighbor

Commandments four through ten are about love for others. When we follow these seven commandments, we follow Jesus' instruction to love our neighbor as we love ourselves. Here is what each of these commandments tells us.

How do the commandments help us follow Jesus' teachings?

The Commandment	What the Commandment Means
4 Honor your father and your mother.	Treat your parents with respect. Show them gratitude and love.
5 You shall not kill.	All human life is sacred, from the moment of conception to natural death. Respect and protect the lives of others and your own life.
6 You shall not commit adultery.	Marriage requires faithful love and commitment between husband and wife.
7 You shall not steal.	Respect the things that belong to others. Do not steal or cheat. Protect the earth's resources and work to preserve them.
8 You shall not bear false witness against your neighbor.	Always be honest and truthful. Do not say untruthful or negative things about others.
9 You shall not covet your neighbor's wife.	Show respect for your own body and the bodies of others.
10 You shall not covet your neighbor's goods.	Do not be jealous of others' possessions. Be thankful for the gifts God has given you.

Live Your Faith

For each of the three commandments below, create a rule children your age can follow at home or at school. Then write a prayer asking God to help you follow the commandments.

Honor your father and mother.

_____

_____

You shall not steal.

_____

_____

You shall not bear false witness against your neighbor.

_____

_____

FAITH FACTS

➧ We must always obey God's laws ahead of any others. If someone in authority over us wants us to do something that goes against God's laws, we have to disobey that person and choose what pleases God.

➧ God created the earth's resources for all people. We have to work to protect God's creation.

➧ We must respect our own reputation and the reputations of others. This means we should not tell negative things about others, even if those things are true.

My Prayer

Dear God, _____

_____

_____

Saints and Holy People

Saint Teresa of Calcutta (1910–1997)

As a young girl, Saint Teresa, commonly called "Mother" Teresa, read about the works of Catholic missionaries in all parts of the world. She knew she wanted to serve others as they did. She became a religious sister and lived in India. At first she served as a teacher in a school for girls. But Teresa felt that God called her to serve the poorest people in India.

With the archbishop's permission, Teresa started a new religious order, called the Missionaries of Charity.

Mother Teresa and her religious sisters worked among poor people in the streets of Calcutta, in India. They founded homes where they could bring the people that lay dying on the city streets. The sisters cared for those people and treated them with love and mercy. The sisters also founded orphanages for the unwanted children of Calcutta. They cared for the children's physical needs. They also educated them, taught them about God, and showed them love and care. Mother Teresa and her sisters cared for those who were abandoned and unloved.

Mother Teresa died in 1997, but the Missionaries of Charity continue to care for the poor around the world. In 2003, Pope John Paul II named Mother Teresa "blessed," and Pope Francis canonized her in 2016.

Catholic Customs   Giving Alms

Ever since the time of the Apostles, the Church has taken care of those who are poor. Today, we can all care for people in need by giving alms, or donating money. When we care for the poor in this way, we show love for our neighbor and love for God. Think about ways you can give alms, such as through special collections at your parish.

Make It Happen

Like the Good Samaritan, Mother Teresa cared for people in need and taught them about God's love. In 1979, Mother Teresa received the Nobel Peace Prize for all she did to serve the poor.

In the ribbon and seal, create an award for caring for those in need. Give your award a name. Tell who will receive the award. Then on the lines below describe how the person showed great love for others.

_____

_____

_____

_____

Reach Out!

Mother Teresa treated every person as her neighbor, especially those who were most in need of love and help.

➡ **How can you follow Mother Teresa's example, and Jesus' message in the Parable of the Good Samaritan?**

We Pray

A Prayer of Loving Service

Father, we honor the heart of your Son, the symbol of perfect love. You call us to follow his example. Teach us to see Christ in the lives of others. Help us to show love for him by loving and serving our brothers and sisters. We ask this through Christ, our Lord. Amen.

—Based on a prayer by Saint Margaret Mary Alacoque

Lesson 16 Review

A **Draw a line** to match each commandment in column A with its number in column B.

Column A

1. You shall not steal.

2. You shall not commit adultery.

3. You shall not covet your neighbor's wife.

4. Honor your father and your mother.

5. You shall not covet your neighbor's goods.

6. You shall not kill.

7. You shall not bear false witness against your neighbor.

Column B

Fourth Commandment

Fifth Commandment

Sixth Commandment

Seventh Commandment

Eighth Commandment

Ninth Commandment

Tenth Commandment

B **Complete** the following sentences.

8. In the Parable of the _____, Jesus taught his followers what it means to love our neighbor.

9. _____ followed Jesus' commandment about loving our neighbor by serving the poor in India.

10. We can show love for our neighbor by giving _____, or donating money for those in need.

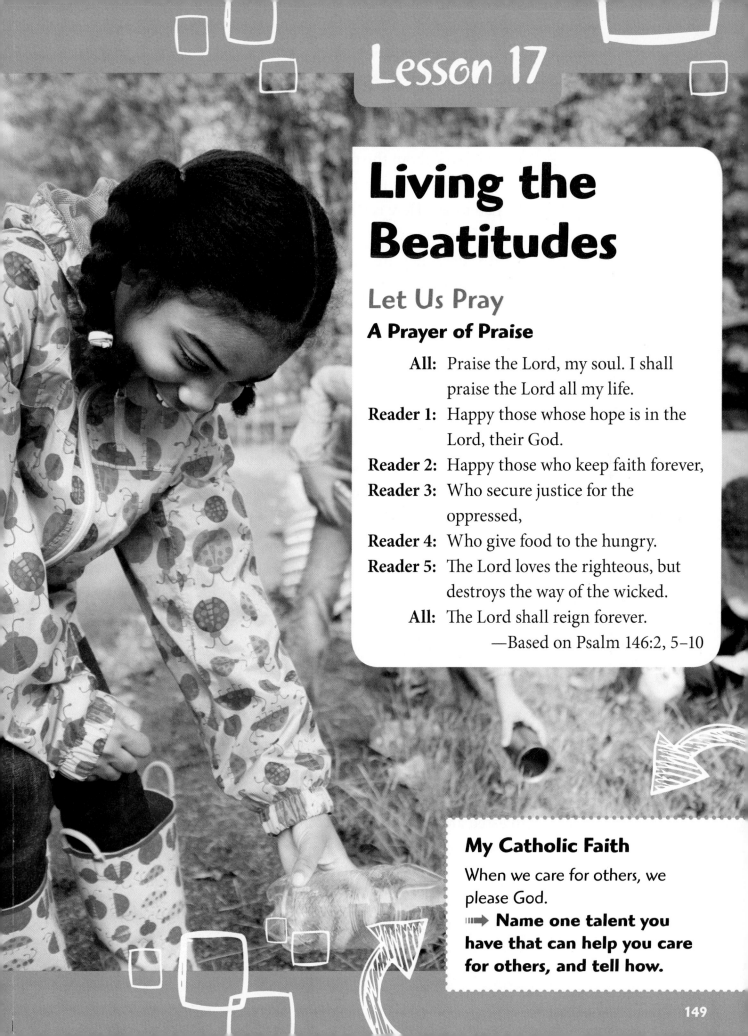

Living the Beatitudes

Let Us Pray

A Prayer of Praise

All: Praise the Lord, my soul. I shall praise the Lord all my life.

Reader 1: Happy those whose hope is in the Lord, their God.

Reader 2: Happy those who keep faith forever,

Reader 3: Who secure justice for the oppressed,

Reader 4: Who give food to the hungry.

Reader 5: The Lord loves the righteous, but destroys the way of the wicked.

All: The Lord shall reign forever.

—Based on Psalm 146:2, 5–10

My Catholic Faith

When we care for others, we please God.

➡ **Name one talent you have that can help you care for others, and tell how.**

Sacred Scripture

You may remember that Jesus didn't start his public ministry until he was about thirty years old. When he did start teaching, great crowds of people followed him! They wanted to hear what he had to say. Here is what Jesus taught about how to live as part of the Kingdom of God. These teachings are called the **Beatitudes**. They are part of a group of Jesus' teachings called the Sermon on the Mount.

Scripture at Mass

The Scripture about the Beatitudes is a Gospel reading we hear at Mass. The Gospel at Mass is read by the priest or by the deacon assisting him.

The Beatitudes

When Jesus saw the crowds, he sat down and began to teach them. He said:

"Blessed are the poor in spirit,
   for theirs is the kingdom of heaven.
Blessed are they who mourn,
   for they will be comforted.
Blessed are the meek,
   for they will inherit the land.
Blessed are they who hunger and thirst for righteousness,
   for they will be satisfied.
Blessed are the merciful,
   for they will be shown mercy.
Blessed are the clean of heart,
   for they will see God.
Blessed are the peacemakers,
   for they will be called children of God.
Blessed are they who are persecuted for the sake of righteousness,
   for theirs is the kingdom of heaven."
   —Matthew 5:3–10

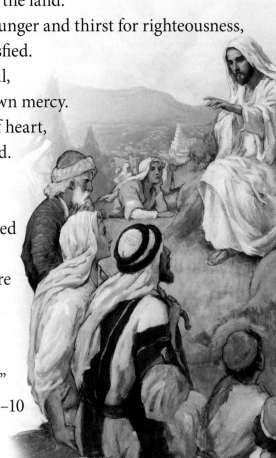

Living the Scripture

Write an acrostic using the word *Beatitudes*. For each letter, write a word or phrase about the Beatitudes. The first *e* is done for you.

_____ **b**

J **e** sus taught us _____

_____ **a** _____

_____ **t** _____

_____ **i** _____

_____ **t** _____

_____ **u** _____

_____ **d** _____

_____ **e** _____

_____ **s** _____

Words to Know

Beatitudes
Jesus' teachings about how to live as part of the Kingdom of God

Our Catholic Tradition

Jesus Teaches Us How to Live

All people like to be happy. God created us that way. When Jesus taught the Beatitudes, he taught us how to find true happiness. Here is what the Beatitudes say.

The Beatitude	What the Beatitude Means
Blessed are the poor in spirit…	Obey God always. Trust in his goodness.
Blessed are they who mourn…	Help those who are sad or suffering.
Blessed are the meek…	Be gentle and patient with others.
Blessed are they who hunger and thirst for righteousness…	Treat all people justly. Help change unjust conditions.
Blessed are the merciful…	Forgive those who have offended or hurt you.
Blessed are the clean of heart…	Be gentle and humble. Love God and love others.
Blessed are the peacemakers…	Work to bring God's peace to others.
Blessed are they who are persecuted for the sake of righteousness…	Do what is right even when it is not popular.

As Jesus explains, happiness comes from loving and trusting in God. It also comes from loving and caring for others. We can care for others by doing **Works of Mercy**. Through these loving acts, we show respect for other people's dignity. The Works of Mercy are divided into these two groups:

The Corporal Works of Mercy These acts have to do with caring for the physical needs of others. They include helping those who are poor and visiting the sick.

The Spiritual Works of Mercy These acts focus on the needs of the heart, mind, and soul. They include praying for others, comforting the suffering, and forgiving those who hurt us.

How can we show love and care for others?

Live Your Faith

What the Beatitudes tell us is different from what people sometimes think brings happiness. By following the Beatitudes, you can experience true happiness. You can also bring happiness to others. Use the chart on the opposite page to remember the Beatitudes and what each one means. Then, for each Beatitude, tell one thing you can do to share happiness. Write one on each flower petal.

Sharing Happiness

Words to Know

Works of Mercy loving acts of caring for the physical and spiritual needs of other people

Saints and Holy People

Saint Rose of Lima (1586–1617)

Rose of Lima was born in Lima, Peru. She showed great love for God even as a young child. Rose wanted to become a nun, but her parents wanted her to marry. They eventually let Rose join the Third Order of Saint Dominic. This meant she could live the life of a religious sister at home with her parents.

Rose put all her trust in God. She only wanted to do what pleased him. She showed love for God through her prayers and by making sacrifices, such as by fasting. Rose also showed love for others by serving those in need. She cared for the poor and sick people of her city, sometimes bringing them to her home to care for them. She sold her needlework and flowers that she grew to support people in need. Rose said, "When we serve the poor and the sick, we serve Jesus."

Rose of Lima followed Jesus' teaching in the Beatitudes. She showed great love for God and trusted in his goodness. She also cared for those who were suffering and worked to bring them comfort.

Saint Rose of Lima is the patron saint of Latin America. We celebrate her feast day on August 23.

Catholic Customs

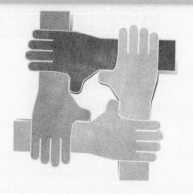

Catholic Social Teaching

The Catholic Church's social teaching tells us how to live lives of holiness in today's world. The bishops of the United States named seven themes of Catholic social teaching. These teachings call us to work for justice and peace in society. We should work to make sure all people have what they need to live with dignity. See page 205 to learn more about Catholic social teaching and ways you can do your part.

Make It Happen

When we live the Beatitudes, we place our trust in God. We also find true happiness by doing what pleases God. In the space below, write two things Saint Rose of Lima did for God. Then write two things you do to please God.

What Saint Rose of Lima Did to Please God	What I Do to Please God

Faith at Home

Find out about a ministry your parish has to care for the poor. For example, maybe your parish runs a food pantry. With a parent or another family member, volunteer to work with this ministry.

We Pray

Prayer of Saint Francis

Lord, make me an instrument of your peace. Where there is hatred, let me sow love; where there is injury, pardon; where there is doubt, faith; where there is despair, hope; where there is darkness, light; and where there is sadness, joy.

O Divine Master, grant that I may not so much seek to be consoled as to console, to be understood as to understand, to be loved as to love; for it is in giving that we receive, it is in pardoning that we are pardoned, and it is in dying that we are born to eternal life.

Lesson 17 Review

A **Complete** the following sentences, using words from the box.

1. The _____ Works of Mercy have to do with caring for the physical needs of others.

2. The _____ Works of Mercy focus on the needs of the heart, mind, and soul.

3. The _____ are Jesus' teachings about how to live as part of the Kingdom of God.

4. _____ call us to work for justice and peace in society.

5. Saint Rose of Lima showed love for God through her prayers and by making

   _____ .

Catholic social teaching
Spiritual
Corporal
sacrifices
Beatitudes

B **Draw a line** to match each Beatitude in column A with its meaning in column B.

Column A

6. Blessed are the poor in spirit…

7. Blessed are they who hunger and thirst for righteousness…

8. Blessed are the merciful…

9. Blessed are the peacemakers…

10. Blessed are they who are persecuted for the sake of righteousness…

Column B

Work to bring God's peace to others.

Obey God always. Trust in his goodness.

Forgive those who have offended or hurt you.

Do what is right even when it is not popular.

Treat all people justly. Help change unjust conditions.

BEING CATHOLIC

God Gave Us the Church and the Sacraments

God created the universe out of love for us. He also created us to live as his children. To guide us in this calling, God gave us the Church. The Church helps us follow Jesus' teachings and live in happiness with God and with one another. We become members of the Church through the Sacraments of Christian Initiation—Baptism, Confirmation, and Eucharist.

Baptism is the basis of our life as Christians. It opens the door for us to receive the other sacraments. Through Baptism we are freed from sin and reborn as children of God. We are united to Christ and become members of the Church.

Confirmation seals our life of faith in Christ. It also strengthens our relationship with Jesus and the Church. Through the Holy Spirit, this sacrament helps us fulfill our mission as Jesus' disciples.

The Eucharist completes our union with Christ. The Eucharist, or Holy Communion, also nourishes our life of faith. The Eucharist has such an important place in our lives as Catholics, the Church calls it the "source and the summit" of Christian life.

The Sacraments in Your Life

Through the Sacraments of Baptism, Confirmation, and Eucharist, we are joined to the Body of Christ, the Church. Describe what this means in your life.

_____

_____

We are nourished by the Eucharist. Tell how receiving Holy Communion regularly can nourish you, or make you spiritually strong.

_____

_____

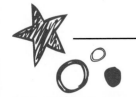

_____

Celebration of the Sacraments of Christian Initiation

Through the Sacraments of Christian Initiation we become members of the Church. Here is some helpful information about each of these sacraments.

Sacrament	Ordinary Minister	Essential Elements	Can it be repeated?
Baptism	bishop, priest, or deacon (In an emergency, anyone can baptize.)	Water poured on the forehead of the candidate, or the immersion of the candidate in water, as the priest says, "I baptize you in the name of the Father, and of the Son and of the Holy Spirit."	No
Confirmation	bishop	The laying on of hands by the bishop, and the anointing on the forehead with Sacred Chrism, or consecrated oil	No
Eucharist	priest or bishop	The words of consecration spoken by the priest, through which the bread and wine become the Body and Blood of Christ	Yes

Baptism and Confirmation mark our souls with a permanent, spiritual sign. Because of this, a person can be baptized and confirmed only once.

The Sacrament of Eucharist is celebrated each time we celebrate Mass. During the Liturgy of the Eucharist, the bread and wine are consecrated by the priest and, through the power of the Holy Spirit, become the Body and Blood of Christ. This action is called transubstantiation. Through transubstantiation, Christ is truly present in his soul and divinity in the consecrated bread and wine.

The Church encourages us to receive Communion frequently, even daily. But we cannot receive Holy Communion if we have committed a mortal sin that we have not confessed. Even if we have not committed a mortal sin, we should celebrate the Sacrament of Penance regularly. This sacrament gives us grace and helps us avoid sin. (See pages 210–211 for how to celebrate the Sacrament of Penance.)

A Communion Prayer

Write a short prayer that you can pray in preparation for receiving Holy Communion.

Dear God, _____

_____

Christian Prayer

It is always possible to pray. It is even a vital necessity. Prayer and Christian life are inseparable. (*CCC*, 2757)

The Lord's Prayer

Our Father, who art in heaven,
hallowed be thy name;
thy kingdom come;
thy will be done
on earth, as it is in heaven.
Give us this day our daily bread;
and forgive us our trespasses
as we forgive those
who trespass against us;
and lead us not into temptation,
but deliver us from evil.
Amen.

Prayer in the Christian Life

Let Us Pray

A Prayer of Trust

All: I love the LORD, who listened....
Who turned an ear to me
on the day I called.

Side 1: Gracious is the LORD and just;
yes, our God is merciful

All: I love the LORD, who listened....
Who turned an ear to me
on the day I called.

Side 2: My soul has been freed from death,
my eyes from tears, my feet
from stumbling.

All: I love the LORD, who listened....
Who turned an ear to me on
the day I called.

—Psalm 116:1–2, 5–6, 8–9

My Catholic Faith

We can talk to God in prayer at any time in our day.

➠ **What is your favorite time of day to pray? How can you talk to God in prayer at that time each day?**

Sacred Scripture

When do you pray? Do you pray to request something for yourself or your family, or to ask for forgiveness for sins you committed? Do you pray to give God thanks and praise? In this Scripture we will read about ten men with a skin disease that Jesus cured. The example of one of those men teaches us that it is important to talk to God in prayer always.

The Cleansing of Ten Lepers

As [Jesus] was entering a village, ten lepers met him. They stood at a distance from him and raised their voice, saying, "Jesus, Master! Have pity on us!" And when he saw them, he said, "Go, show yourselves to the priests." As they were going they were cleansed. And one of them, realizing he had been healed, returned, glorifying God in a loud voice; and he fell at the feet of Jesus and thanked him. He was a Samaritan. Jesus said in reply, "Ten were cleansed, were they not? Where are the other nine? Has none but this foreigner returned to give thanks to God?" Then he said to him, "Stand up and go; your faith has saved you."

—Luke 17:12–19

More Scripture on Prayer

➡ The Parable of the Persistent Widow — Luke 18:1–8

➡ Jesus Teaches about Praying in Private — Matthew 6:5–8

➡ Daniel and the Lion's Den — Daniel 6:6–23

Living the Scripture

The Scripture passage about Jesus curing ten lepers teaches us that we should not forget to pray. We can talk to God in prayer using these forms of prayer.

blessing — Prayers of blessing recognize that God gives us all our blessings, and that because of that, we can bless him in return.

petition — In prayers of petition, we ask God for something for ourselves, such as help in doing well on a test.

intercession — Prayers of intercession ask God for something for someone else, such as healing for a relative who is sick.

thanksgiving — In prayers of thanksgiving, we thank God for his goodness or for specific gifts he has given us.

praise — In prayers of praise, we express our love for God.

Choose one of these types of prayer, and write a one-sentence prayer addressed to God. Then draw a picture to go with your prayer.

Dear God,

_____

_____

_____

_____

God Calls Us to Pray

When you talk to a friend, you do some talking and some listening, right? This is also how prayer works. In prayer, you talk to God and listen to him.

When we pray, we raise our minds and hearts to God. That means we focus on God, to allow him to speak to our hearts.

Saint Paul said, "Pray without ceasing" (1 Thessalonians 5:17). This means that along with praying with words, you can give praise to God through your actions, and by being aware of his presence.

Prayer with words includes praying the Our Father, or talking to God in your own words. But you can also pray without words. Ways to pray without words include meditation and contemplation. **Meditation** is thinking about God and his presence in our lives. Sometimes people read from Scripture or look at holy images to help them meditate. **Contemplation** is similar to meditation, but this way of praying involves just being fully in the presence of God. In contemplation we focus on our feelings of love for God.

Sometimes praying is not easy. We might feel like God is far away. Even the saints felt this way sometimes. If you have this feeling, the best thing to do is to just keep on praying and trust that God is near.

> How is prayer like talking to a friend?

> How can we pray without words?

> What should we do when praying is hard?

Live Your Faith

Use the image below to pray a prayer of meditation. Begin by looking at the image. Take your time and let your mind and heart take in what the image communicates to you. If you become distracted, just keep going back to the image and focusing on it. After you have taken quiet time to reflect, use words to speak to God.

Words to Know

meditation
thinking about God and his presence in our lives

contemplation
a way of praying by simply being in the presence of God and focusing on our love for him

Express in prayer the feelings and thoughts you had while focusing on the image.

_____

_____

_____

Saints and Holy People

Saint Paul Miki and Companions (d. 1597)

In the sixteenth century, missionaries traveled to Japan to teach about the Catholic faith. Over the years, thousands of Japanese people were baptized and became Catholic. They included a boy named Paul Miki and his family.

At first the Japanese emperor allowed Catholics to practice their faith. But over time, he became suspicious of them. He began to persecute Catholics, and they often had to practice their faith in secret. In 1596, the emperor sentenced twenty-six Catholics to death. The group included priests and men studying to become priests, along with lay people and children. Paul Miki, who was studying to be a priest, was among the group.

The group had to march to the city of Nagasaki, where they would be crucified. Along the way Paul and his companions continued to pray and preach to the crowds about Jesus.

When Paul was on the cross, he said, "After Christ's example, I forgive the emperor and my persecutors. I pray that they will be baptized." The entire group prayed together in their last moments before death.

Paul and his companions, called the Martyrs of Nagasaki, were canonized in 1862. We celebrate their feast day on February 6.

Catholic Customs — *Lectio Divina*

A popular way to meditate is through a kind of prayer called *lectio divina* (lect-see-oh di-vee-na). *Lectio divina* means "holy reading." This is one of the oldest forms of Christian prayer. *Lectio divina* involves four steps: 1) reading a Scripture passage; 2) repeating the passage; 3) thinking about what to say to God in response to the passage; and 4) reflecting on the question: "What is God saying to me?"

Make It Happen

It is important to pray always, even when our circumstances make it difficult. When is it easy to pray? At what times is prayer difficult?

Describe a situation when prayer is easy. Then describe a situation when praying is not easy, and tell why. Write one thing you can do to pray even when it is difficult.

It is easy to pray when _____

_____

It is not easy to pray when _____

_____

What I can do to pray even when it isn't easy: _____

_____

Reach Out

How much do you know about Christians living in other countries? Choose a country in a faraway part of the world and learn about the challenges for Christians who live there. Make a commitment to pray for them regularly.

We Pray

A Meditation Prayer

In Chapter 8 of the Gospel of Matthew we read about Jesus calming a storm at sea (verses 23–27). When the storm blew in, the disciples were frightened. Jesus calmed the storm and took away their fear.

Close your eyes and focus on what you hear as your teacher reads the Scripture from Matthew's Gospel.

Lesson 18 Review

A **Complete** each sentence with the letter of the correct word from the box.

1. _____ requires talking as well as listening to God.

2. _____ is thinking about God and his presence in our lives.

3. _____ is a way of praying by simply being in the presence of God.

4. _____ means holy reading.

5. Saint Paul Miki and his companions are known as the Martyrs of _____ .

a. Contemplation
b. Prayer
c. *Lectio Divina*
d. Nagasaki
e. Meditation

B **Draw a line** to match each type of prayer to the right description.

6. We recognize that God gives us all our blessings and we bless him in return.

7. We ask God for something for ourselves.

8. We ask God for something for someone else.

9. We thank God for his goodness.

10. We simply express our love for God.

Blessing

Praise

Thanksgiving

Petition

Intercession

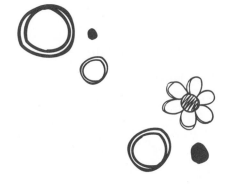

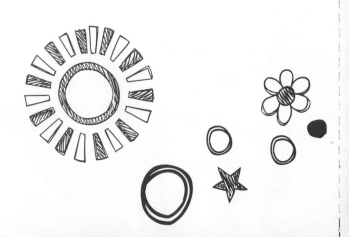

The Lord's Prayer

Let Us Pray

Psalm 23

The LORD is my shepherd;
 there is nothing I lack.
In green pastures he makes me lie down;
 to still waters he leads me;
 he restores my soul.
He guides me along right paths
 for the sake of his name.
Even though I walk through the shadow of the valley of death,
 I will fear no evil, for you are with me;
 your rod and your staff comfort me.
You set a table before me
 in front of my enemies;
You anoint my head with oil;
 my cup overflows.
Indeed, goodness and mercy will pursue me
 all the days of my life;
I will dwell in the house of the LORD.
 for endless days.

My Catholic Faith

We often address God as our Father.
➡ **How does it make you feel to talk to God as Father?**

Sacred Scripture

Sometimes it's hard to find the right words to pray. Even Jesus' disciples sometimes did not have the right words for speaking to God. They asked Jesus to teach them to pray. In response, Jesus taught them the Lord's Prayer. You might know this prayer as the Our Father.

The Lord's Prayer

Jesus said to his disciples,
"This is how you are to pray:
    Our Father in heaven,
        hallowed be your name,
        your kingdom come,
        your will be done,
           on earth as it is in heaven.
    Give us today our daily bread;
    and forgive us our debts,
        as we forgive our debtors;
    and do not subject us to the final test,
        but deliver us from the evil
        one."

—Matthew 6:9–13

Scripture at Mass

This Scripture is the Gospel reading during a special rite called the Presentation of the Lord's Prayer. This presentation is part of the Rite of Christian Initiation of Adults (RCIA). We also pray the Lord's Prayer at every Mass during the Liturgy of the Eucharist.

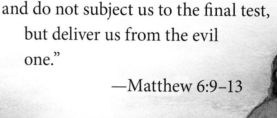

Living the Scripture

Imagine being present with the disciples who asked Jesus to teach them to pray. What would you ask Jesus to teach you about praying?

_____

_____

The Lord's Prayer, which we also call the Our Father, is a prayer that Jesus himself taught us. How does knowing this make you feel about praying this prayer?

_____

_____

_____

Read the words of the Lord's Prayer slowly and reflectively. Then choose a part of the prayer to illustrate in the space below. Write the words that you are illustrating at the bottom of your drawing.

_____

Our Catholic Tradition

Jesus Teaches Us to Pray

When Jesus taught us the Lord's Prayer, he taught us that we can call God "Father." The Lord's Prayer is composed of seven petitions, or requests to God. These seven petitions contain a summary of the whole Gospel. Here is what the opening and the petitions mean.

Our Father who art in Heaven This opening shows that we know God as a loving Father, and that we are his children. By saying that God is "in Heaven," it also praises his glory.

The first three petitions are focused on giving glory to God. The next four petitions have to do with our needs and the needs of all people. Let us look at what each of the petitions means.

What are the seven requests we make in the Lord's Prayer?

1 **hallowed be thy name** *Hallowed* means holy. We pray that God's name will always be kept holy by all people.

2 **Thy kingdom come** We pray that God will rule over all people.

3 **Thy will be done on earth as it is in heaven** We ask God to help us live according to his will. We ask him to help us always accept his will.

4 **Give us this day our daily bread** We pray that all people will have all that they need to live, like food and shelter.

5 **and forgive us our trespasses as we forgive those who trespass against us** We ask God to forgive us when we sin, and to help us forgive those who hurt us.

6 **and lead us not into temptation** We ask God to help us avoid sin and always choose what is good.

7 **but deliver us from evil** We pray with the whole Church that God will save us from sin.

Live Your Faith

Read the following statements. Put an X in the boxes next to statements that do not match any part of the Lord's Prayer. For the remaining statements, tell which petition each matches by putting the number of the petition in the box. One has been done for you.

○ I am angry with my brother for the mean thing he said to me yesterday.

⑦ Dear Lord, as your Church, we ask you to lead us to eternity with you.

○ Lord, help the people who lost their homes in the hurricane.

○ Lord, fill the world with your love and goodness.

○ Even though I wanted a different answer to my prayer, I accept the way God responded.

○ I only speak God's name with love and respect.

○ God, I need your help staying out of trouble.

○ Lord, I'm sorry I was not kind to my new classmate today.

○ Dear Lord, I will only be happy if you answer my prayers the way I want.

FAITH FACTS

➡ When we pray the Lord's Prayer, we call God our Father, just like Jesus did. Through the prayer, we are united with God the Father and with his Son, Jesus Christ.

➡ When we pray to God as our Father, we pray with all people and for all people, that they may know the one true God.

➡ Because this prayer expresses all we need to say to God so perfectly, it is the model prayer of the Church.

Saints and Holy People

Saint Thomas Aquinas (1225–1274)

Thomas Aquinas was born to a noble family in Italy. From a very young age Thomas showed great intelligence. But he always knew that his mind was a gift from God. He wanted to use it to bring glory to God.

When Thomas was eighteen, he met a group of men called the Dominicans. Their religious order had recently been founded by Saint Dominic. Thomas knew he wanted to be a priest, and he wanted to join this religious order.

Thomas joined the Dominicans and went to the University of Paris to study theology—which is the study of the nature of God. Thomas Aquinas became a brilliant writer and teacher. He wrote so well about God that people all over the world have studied his books for hundreds of years. His writings have helped us learn about God and about our faith. Thomas Aquinas explained that everything in the universe exists because of God. He also helped us understand that we can use our minds to know God, and that we can know God through the wonderful world he created.

Saint Thomas Aquinas is one of the great teachers of the Church. He was named a **Doctor of the Church** in 1567. We celebrate his feast day on January 28.

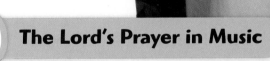

Catholic Customs   The Lord's Prayer in Music

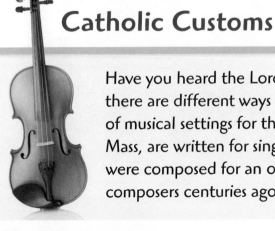

Have you heard the Lord's Prayer sung at Mass? Have you noticed that there are different ways to sing this prayer? Actually, there are hundreds of musical settings for the Lord's Prayer. Some, like the versions we sing at Mass, are written for singing by the people gathered for the liturgy. Others were composed for an orchestra to perform. Some were written by famous composers centuries ago.

Make It Happen

Saint Thomas Aquinas had a brilliant mind. He used it to write and teach about God. Name a special gift or talent God has given you. Tell at least one way you can use this talent to help others know about God.

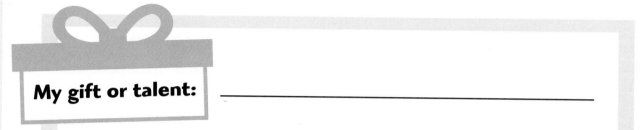

My gift or talent: _____

How I can use it to help others know God:

_____

_____

_____

Words to Know

Doctor of the Church
a title the Church gives to people whose writings have helped others understand the faith

Faith at Home

Our family is the first place we can learn to pray. It's especially important for a family to pray together each day. If your family doesn't already pray together each day, maybe you can start the tradition. You can start out by getting everyone to join in praying the Lord's Prayer.

We Pray

The Lord's Prayer

Our Father who art in heaven,
hallowed be thy name.
Thy kingdom come.
Thy will be done on earth, as it is
    in heaven.
Give us this day our daily bread,
and forgive us our trespasses,
as we forgive those who trespass
    against us,
and lead us not into temptation,
but deliver us from evil. Amen.

Lesson 19 Review

A Fill in the circle beside the correct answer.

1. The Lord's Prayer is a summary of the _____.
   - ○ Old Testament
   - ○ writings of Saint Thomas Aquinas
   - ○ whole Gospel

2. The _____ of the Lord's Prayer is/are focused on giving glory to God.
   - ○ last petition
   - ○ fourth petition
   - ○ first three petitions

3. The _____ of the Lord's Prayer have to do with human needs for ourselves and the whole human family.
   - ○ last four petitions
   - ○ last two petitions
   - ○ first three petitions

B Match each petition of the Lord's Prayer in column A with its meaning in column B by writing the letter in the space provided.

Column A

4. _____ hallowed be thy name

5. _____ Thy kingdom come

6. _____ Thy will be done on earth as it is in heaven

7. _____ Give us this day our daily bread

8. _____ and forgive us our trespasses as we forgive those who trespass against us

9. _____ and lead us not into temptation

10. _____ but deliver us from evil

Column B

a. We pray with the whole Church that God will save us from sin.

b. We ask God to help us live according to his will and to always accept his will.

c. We pray that God's name will always be kept holy by all people.

d. We pray that all people will have all that they need to live, like food and shelter.

e. We ask God to help us avoid sin and always choose what is good.

f. We ask God to forgive our sins and to help us forgive those who hurt us.

g. We pray that God will rule over all people.

Praying with Devotions

Let Us Pray

A Prayer of Thanksgiving

Reader 1: God indeed is my salvation;
I am confident and unafraid.

All: I give you thanks, O LORD.

Reader 2: For the LORD is my strength
and my might,
and he has been my salvation.

All: I give you thanks, O LORD.

Reader 3: Give thanks to the LORD,
acclaim his name;
among the nations make known
his deeds.

All: I give you thanks, O LORD.

—Isaiah 12:1, 2, 4, 5

My Catholic Faith

Like a good friend, God is always
happy to hear from us.

➡ **How often do you talk to
God in prayer? How can you
communicate with him more
often?**

Sacred Scripture

At the Sermon on the Mount, Jesus taught his disciples the Beatitudes. He also taught them about prayer. The Lord's Prayer, which you learned about in Lesson 19, was part of that teaching. Jesus also taught the disciples about how God answers our prayers.

The Answer to Prayers

Jesus said to his disciples,

"Ask and it will be given to you: seek and you will find; knock and the door will be opened to you. For everyone who asks, receives; and the one who seeks, finds; and to the one who knocks, the door will be opened."

He then went on:

"Which one of you would hand [your child] a stone when he asks for a loaf of bread, or a snake when he asks for a fish? If you then, who are wicked, know how to give good gifts to your children, how much more will your heavenly Father give good things to those who ask him."

—Matthew 7:7–11

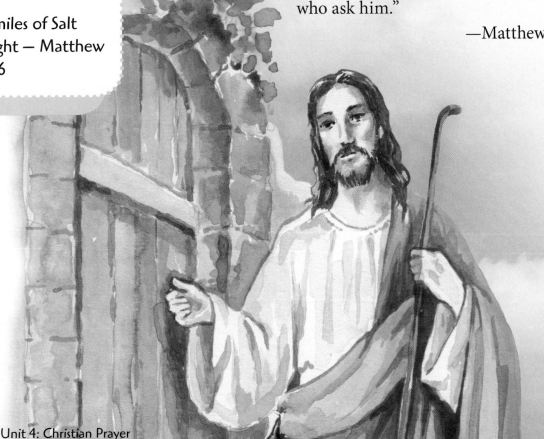

More Scripture from the Sermon on the Mount

➠ Do Not Judge Others — Matthew 7:1–5

➠ The Golden Rule — Matthew 7:12

➠ Similes of Salt and Light — Matthew 5:13–16

Living the Scripture

The Scripture passage about how God answers our prayers tells us that he always answers us. After all, Jesus said, "Ask and you will receive." Does this mean that if you pray for a new video game or a new pair of shoes God will see to it that you get them? Does it mean that God will always answer your prayers by giving you just what you ask for?

When we pray, it's important to remember that God's answer to our prayers. . .

- is not always obvious to us.
- does not always come right away.
- may not be the answer we prayed for.

No matter how God answers our prayers, we have to trust in his love and accept his will.

Describe a time when you prayed for something and God answered you in a different way than you expected.

_____

_____

_____

Imagine that a friend is upset about a problem and feels that God is not listening to his or her prayers. What advice would you give your friend?

_____

_____

Our Catholic Tradition

Praying with Devotions

There are many different ways to communicate with God in prayer. We can pray at Mass and in other liturgies. We can pray by singing and through gestures. We can pray using the traditional prayers of the Church, such as the Our Father and the Hail Mary. We can also pray using popular **devotions**. You probably know at least one devotion, such as the Rosary.

Catholics have used devotions as a way to pray since the time of the early Church. Over time, Catholics in different cultures developed their own devotions. But some devotions are practiced by Catholics around the world. These include:

- the Rosary, a devotion to Mary,
- the Stations of the Cross, in which we reflect on the events of Jesus' Passion and death,
- praying **novenas**,
- making pilgrimages, such as to an important shrine, and
- receiving blessed ashes on Ash Wednesday.

Devotions that are common to specific cultures include the Corpus Christi processions to honor Christ in the Eucharist. Another is the devotion to Our Lady of Guadalupe. This devotion originated in Mexico.

> What are some ways we can pray?

> What are some devotions Catholics pray?

Live Your Faith

How often do you talk to your best friend? You probably talk almost every day. How often do you talk to God? Like a best friend, God is always happy to hear from you. Think about some things you can talk to God about. You can tell him things that make you happy, and things that make you sad. You can tell him your worries, and you can ask him for help. You can also thank him for his goodness.

On the sticky note, write a list of things you can talk to God about. Then use the notepaper to write to God about one of those things.

FAITH FACTS

➡ Although the Mass and the sacraments are still our most important way to pray, devotions also enrich our Catholic faith.

➡ The Church encourages devotional practices that help us proclaim our faith and strengthen our relationship with God.

Words to Know

devotions
forms of prayer that are separate from the Mass and the sacraments

novena
a series of prayers for a specific intention prayed over nine days

Saints and Holy People

Our Lady of Guadalupe

On December 9, 1531, a man named Juan Diego saw the Blessed Mother on a hill in Mexico City. Mary appeared as a young pregnant native woman. She asked Juan to go to the bishop and ask him to build a church in her honor. The bishop did not believe what Juan told him. He asked him for proof.

On December 12 Mary appeared to Juan Diego again. She asked him to go to the hill where she first appeared to him and gather flowers to bring to the bishop. Juan Diego did as Mary instructed. Even though flowers did not normally bloom at that time, he found roses that he could collect. He wrapped them in his tilma, or cloak, and brought them to the bishop. When he unfolded his tilma, he and the bishop were amazed to see Mary's image imprinted on it. Mary looked just as Juan Diego had described her.

The bishop knew this was a miracle. He ordered a church to be built where Mary had appeared.

Today millions of people make a pilgrimage to the Basilica of Our Lady of Guadalupe in Mexico City each year. Our Lady of Guadalupe, called *Nuestra Señora de Guadalupe,* is the most popular devotion among Mexican people.

Catholic Customs   Praying Novenas

Praying a novena is a Catholic devotion. The word *novena* comes from the Latin word for nine. A novena is prayed over nine days. Novenas are usually prayers of petition. That means they are prayed with a request to God for help with a specific need. Most novenas are addressed to Mary or a saint, asking them to intercede for us, or talk to God on our behalf. One popular Marian novena is the Miraculous Medal novena. The design from the Miraculous Medal is shown at left.

Make It Happen

Design a prayer card to honor Mary. On the left side, draw an image of Mary. On the right side, write a prayer to Mary in your words.

Reach Out!

Think about someone you know who is going through a difficult time, such as because of illness. Choose a devotion, such as the Rosary, and pray it for that person.

We Pray

Prayer to Our Lady of Guadalupe

Our Lady of Guadalupe, help everyone who calls on you in their time of need.

Hear our prayers and our petitions, especially for (*mention your request*). Obtain for us from your most holy Son the grace of keeping our faith, hope in the midst of the hard times of life, burning charity, and the precious gift of final perseverance. Amen.

A **Complete** the crossword puzzle.

Down

1. Our Lady of Guadalupe is the most popular devotion among the people of _____.

2. Our Lady of Guadalupe appeared to _____.

3. The _____ is a devotion to Mary in which we reflect on events in her life and the life of Jesus.

4. No matter how God answers our prayers, we have to trust in his love and accept his _____.

6. Jesus said, "_____ and the door will be opened to you."

10. When we pray the _____ we reflect on the events of Jesus' Passion and death.

Across

5. Jesus said, "_____ and you will find."

7. _____ are separate from Mass and the sacraments but are an important form of prayer.

8. A _____ is a series of prayers prayed over nine days.

9. Jesus said, "_____ and it will be given to you."

BEING CATHOLIC

Sent Forth to Be Disciples

What groups do you belong to aside from your school? Maybe you are part of your school band, or a sports team, or a service group at your school. What happened when you signed up to be part of the group and were accepted? Did you participate in the group's activities?

When we join any group, our goal is usually to become active members of the group. We want to do our part, and to contribute to the group's mission. It is the same way with the Church. When we celebrate the Sacraments of Christian Initiation, we become full members of the Church. As members, we have to participate in the Church's mission.

Becoming members of the Church takes a commitment. First, we have to make a commitment to truly live as followers of Christ. We also have to commit to learning about our faith and truly understanding the meaning of the sacraments. (Of course, if we are baptized as infants, our parents make the commitment for us. But for the other sacraments, it is up to us.)

Invitation to Discipleship

Create a sign inviting children your age to be disciples of Jesus. Be sure your sign tells why being Jesus' disciple will be rewarding. Also tell what is required for being a disciple. Decorate and color your sign.

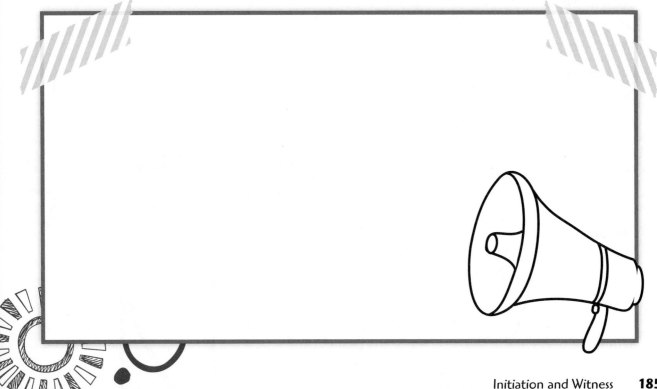

We Are Jesus' Disciples

Being a member of the Church means we have a friendship with Jesus. Like with any friendship, our relationship with Jesus requires something of us.

First, our relationship with Jesus means we have to keep our friendship strong by talking to Jesus regularly. We can do this by praying every day, by participating in the sacraments, and by attending Mass on Sundays and Holy Days of Obligation.

Our friendship with Jesus also means that we have to be willing to make sacrifices. For example, sometimes we might face temptation or pressure from others to do things that hurt our friendship with Jesus. At these times, we have to make choices that honor our friendship with Jesus.

Our friendship also means we must do as Jesus teaches. Jesus said, "I call you friends if you do as I command you" (John 15:15). What did Jesus command his disciples? One command was to go and teach all people about him. This is our command, too. We can teach others about Jesus through our words and our example. We can do this by serving others and living as Jesus teaches every day.

The Path of Discipleship

Take steps as Jesus' disciple. Color in yellow each stone that tells a way to live as Jesus' disciple. Color the other stones black. Color in the rest of your picture.

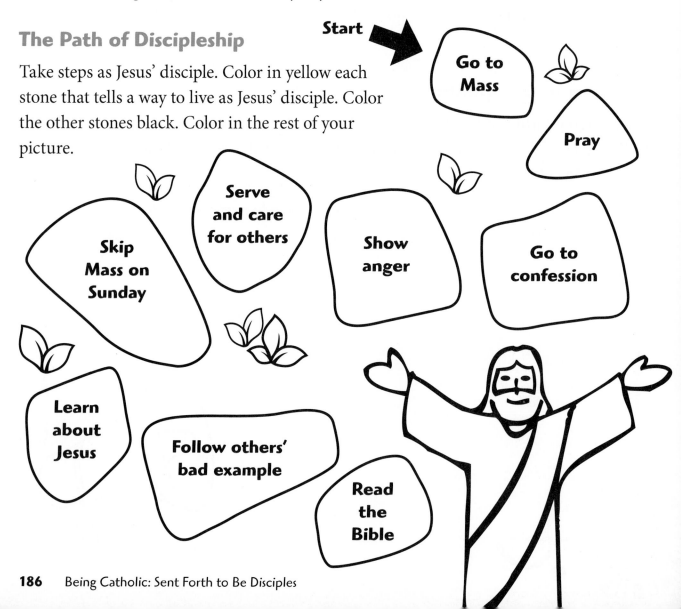

End-of-Year Review

A **Complete** the following sentences, using words from the box.

1. Sacred Scripture and Sacred _____ must be understood together.

2. The _____ is the Third Divine Person of the Blessed Trinity.

3. At _____ the Apostles began their work of evangelization.

4. We become members of the Church through the Sacraments of Christian _____.

5. God created the universe out of _____ for us.

6. God created us in his own _____ and likeness.

7. Adam and Eve's sin and the way it affects all people is called _____.

8. A _____ is a person who answers God's call to help people all over the world know about Jesus.

9. The _____ are God's laws that tell us what is required to love God and others.

10. The _____ are Jesus' teachings about how to live as part of the Kingdom of God.

Beatitudes
missionary
image
Ten Commandments
Tradition
Pentecost
love
Holy Spirit
Initiation
Original Sin

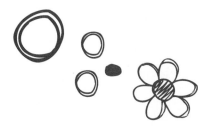

B Fill in the circle beside the correct answer.

11. The way God makes himself and his plan for all people known to us is called _____.

    ○ faith   ○ Divine Revelation   ○ Sacred Scripture

12. Jesus is the _____ Divine Person of the Blessed Trinity.

    ○ First   ○ Second   ○ Third

13. The celebration of the Eucharist is called _____.

    ○ Eucharistic Adoration   ○ Mass   ○ the Blessed Sacrament

14. Baptized men are ordained as bishops, priests, or deacons in the Sacrament of _____.

    ○ Eucharist   ○ Holy Orders   ○ Matrimony

15. In the Sacrament of _____ a baptized man and a baptized woman make a lifelong commitment to love each other and care for their children.

    ○ Eucharist   ○ Holy Orders   ○ Matrimony

16. Our God-given freedom and ability to make choices is called _____.

    ○ free will   ○ temptation   ○ virtues

17. The last _____ commandments guide us in how we are to treat others.

    ○ five   ○ six   ○ seven

18. _____ requires talking as well as listening to God.

    ○ Prayer   ○ Evangelization   ○ Teaching

19. The Lord's Prayer is a summary of the _____.

    ○ Old Testament   ○ whole Gospel   ○ writings of Saint Thomas Aquinas

20. The _____ petitions of the Lord's Prayer contain a summary of all we need as Christians.

    ○ six   ○ seven   ○ eight

C **Match** each term in column B with its definition in column A by writing the correct letter in the space provided.

Column A

21. _____ the mystery of the one God in three Divine Persons

22. _____ the full joy of living eternally in God's presence

23. _____ the name for the four characteristics that identify Christ's Church

24. _____ the mystery of the Son of God becoming man to save all people

25. _____ the sacrament that gives us God's forgiveness after we have sinned

26. _____ the first sacrament that unites us to Christ

27. _____ the sacrament that gives God's grace to those who are suffering in mind, body, or spirit

28. _____ our spiritual Mother and the Mother of the Church

29. _____ acts that show care for others

30. _____ the spiritual part of a human that lives forever

Column B

a. the Blessed Trinity

b. Baptism

c. Incarnation

d. Marks of the Church

e. Mary

f. Heaven

g. soul

h. Penance

i. Anointing of the Sick

j. Works of Mercy

D **Complete** the following sentences, using words from the box.

31. The Church helps us understand everything in the

    _____ and what it means for

    our lives.

32. On the night before he died, Jesus established the

    Sacrament of the _____ .

33. _____ are separate from

    Mass and the sacraments but are an important form of

    Catholic prayer.

34. Mary was an important part of God's plan for our

    _____ .

35. The _____ is the Body

    of Christ.

36. The _____ and the Stations of the Cross are

    devotions prayed by Catholics all over the world.

37. The basic forms of Christian _____ include

    blessing, petition, intercession, thanksgiving, and praise.

38. We can show love for others by giving _____ , or donating

    money for those in need.

39. The first three _____ tell us how to be

    faithful to God.

40. Jesus taught us that God is a loving _____ .

Church
Bible
devotions
Father
commandments
Eucharist
salvation
alms
prayer
Rosary

Catholic Prayers and Devotions

Sign of the Cross

In the name of the Father,

and of the Son,

and of the Holy Spirit.

Amen.

Signum Crucis
(SIHG num)   (KROO chees)

In   nomine   Patris,
(ihn)   (NOH mee nay)   (PAH trees)

et   Filii,
(et)   (FEE lee ee)

et   Spiritus   Sancti.
(et)   (SPEE ree toos)   (SAHNK tee)

Amen.
(AH men)

Glory Be

Doxologia Minor
(dahx oh loh GEE ah) *(MEE nor)*

Glory Be	Doxologia Minor
Glory be to the Father,	Gloria Patri, *(GLOH ree ah)* *(PAH tree)*
and to the Son,	et Filio, *(et)* *(FEE lee oh)*
and to the Holy Spirit.	et Spiritui Sancto. *(et)* *(spee REE too ee)* *(SAHNK toh)*
As it was in the beginning,	Sicut erat in principio, *(SEE koot)* *(AIR aht)* *(ihn)* *(prihn CHEE pee oh)*
is now,	et nunc, et semper, *(et)* *(noonk)* *(et)* *(SEM pair)*
and will be forever.	et in saecula saeculorum. *(et)* *(ihn)* *(SAY koo lah)* *(say koo LOR um)*
Amen.	Amen. *(AH men)*

Bible Timeline

Egypt dus BC	In the Promised Land 1250 BC – 1050 BC	Kingdoms of Judah and Israel 1050 BC – 587 BC	The Ex 58

In the Promised Land 1250 BC – 1050 BC

Kingdoms of Judah and Israel 1050 BC – 587 BC

The Ex 58

---

are ypt

lead the lavery

to Egypt h free the

y Moses, ypt and reach the nd

od gives ments to t Sinai

Moses dies, and God calls Joshua to lead the Israelites into the Promised Land

Each of the Twelve Tribes settles a section of the land

God sends warriors called judges to help the Israelites defend the land against invaders

---

Saul is anointed the first king of Israel

David, the next king, is a powerful ruler; he unites the Twelve Tribes into one kingdom

David's son, Solomon, builds the Temple in Jerusalem

The Kingdom is split into two: Israel and Judah

As God's people turn away from him, God sends prophets to call them back to himself

Prophets like Amos, Isaiah, and Jeremiah tell the people to honor God and live justly

---

Israel conquere and the Te many Juc captiv

After fift in Babylor to return rebui

The Mac with Syr vandalize Maccab rededic

Esther sav Persia f

Jacob

Jacob, renamed Israel, was the grandson of Abraham. Jacob had twelve sons, each of whom began one of the Twelve Tribes of Israel. Jacob is honored as one of the fathers of the Chosen People, the Jews.

Moses

Moses grew up in the royal palace of Egypt. Yet, he never forgot that he was a Jew. God called him to free the Jews from slavery in Egypt, and Moses, under God's guidance, led his people to freedom.

Deborah

Deborah was a prophetess in Israel and the only female judge mentioned in the Bible. With her support, the army of the Israelites won victory over their enemies. She is called "the mother of Israel."

Solomon

King Solomon was David's son. Solomon asked God for the gift of wisdom, and God rewarded him not only with wisdom, but with riches and power. Solomon built the first Temple, but did not remain faithful to God.

Isaiah

Isaiah was a prophet in the Kingdom of Judah. The Book of Isaiah includes prophecies of the coming Messiah. In the midst of frequent wars and exile, these prophecies gave encouragement to the people.

Esther

Esther was the Jewish Queen of Persia. When the Jews of Persia were threatened with extermination, Esther's influence with the king saved them. All Jews celebrate this event on the feast of Purim.

New Testament

Mary

Mary, the first disciple of Jesus, is the Mother of God. She loved and cared for Jesus, followed him to Calvary, and was present at Pentecost. She was assumed into Heaven, where she intercedes for us.

John the Baptist

John, the cousin of Jesus, called the people to a baptism of repentance and pointed out Jesus, the Messiah. John was imprisoned for denouncing King Herod's immorality and was later beheaded.

Jesus

The Word of God and Second Person of the Trinity became man and was given the name Jesus, meaning "God saves." He suffered death on the Cross, rose again, and lives forever as our Savior and Redeemer.

Peter and the Apostles

Peter led the Apostles and became the first Pope. The other Apostles are Andrew, James, John, Philip, Bartholomew, Thomas, Matthew, Simon, Jude, James the Less, and Judas (later replaced by Matthias).

Mary Magdalene

Mary of Magdala was healed of an emotional sickness by Jesus. She became his disciple. She stood by Jesus at the Cross and she was one of the first to see him after his Resurrection.

Paul

Paul, a follower of the Old Law, persecuted the first Christians. But after Jesus spoke to him in a vision, Paul was converted and began to preach the way of Christ. We still read his Letters today.

Primeval History
Creation to about 2100 BC

God creates Adam and Eve
and all the world

Adam and Eve disobey
God and have to leave the
Garden of Eden

Cain kills his brother Abel

God sends the
Great Flood, but he saves
Noah and his family

The Patriarchs
2100 BC to 1700 BC

God makes a covenant with
Abraham and Sarah

Abraham and Sarah have a
son, named Isaac

Isaac's son Jacob receives his
brother Esau's birthright and
becomes patriarch

Jacob's son Joseph is sold into
slavery in Egypt; he saves his
family from famine

Jacob's sons become the
Patriarchs, called the Twelve
Tribes of Israel

Enslavement i
and the Ex
1700 BC to 12?

The Israelite:
enslaved in E

God calls Moses to
Israelites out of

God sends plagues
to make the Phara(
Israelites

The Israelites, led
journey out of E(
cross the Red Sea to
Promised L

On the journey, (
the Ten Command
Moses on Mour

Adam and Eve

Adam and Eve are our first parents. Adam means "of the earth," and Eve means "mother of all the living." In the Book of Genesis, Adam and Eve disobey God and commit the original (first) sin.

Noah

In the Book of Genesis, Noah is shown to be faithful to God. God instructed Noah to build the ark to save his family from the Flood. When the Flood ended, God sent a rainbow as a sign of his love.

Abraham

Abraham is "our father in faith" because he listened to God. With faith in God's promise, Abraham took his family to a faraway land. God promised to be with Abraham's descendants forever.

Samson

Samson was dedicated to God from his birth. He was very strong, and used his strength to serve God's people. But he was weakened by his enemies. He was killed while destroying a pagan temple.

Samuel

Samuel was a prophet. As a young teen, he had heard God's voice in the Temple. When the people asked for a king, Samuel disagreed, but he anointed the first two kings of Israel, Saul and David.

David

As the second king of Israel, David, despite his faults, trusted in God. David is credited with writing much of the Book of Psalms. God promised that from David's line would come the Messiah.

le and Return
BC – AD 1

and Judah are
d, and Jerusalem
mple are destroyed;
eans are taken in
ty in Babylon

years a new king
allows the people
to Jerusalem and
d the Temple

cabees do battle
an invaders, who
the Temple; the
ees reclaim and
ate the Temple

es the Israelites in
om being killed

The Life of Jesus
3 BC – AD 30

The Incarnation – Jesus is born

Mary and Joseph take Jesus to Egypt to escape Herod's order to kill all firstborn sons

Jesus performs his first miracle at the wedding feast at Cana

Jesus calls the first disciples, Peter and Andrew

Jesus gives us the Eucharist at the Last Supper

Jesus dies on the Cross

The Resurrection – Three days after his death, Jesus rises from the dead

The Ascension – Jesus returns to his Father in Heaven

The Early Church
AD 30 – AD 100

Pentecost – Fifty days after Jesus' Resurrection the Holy Spirit descends on the Apostles and Mary

The Apostles begin preaching the Good News

Saul, an enemy of the followers of Jesus, meets Jesus and becomes a Christian; he is then known as Paul

Paul and the other Apostles travel to teach the Good News; they start new Christian communities

The Church continues to grow throughout the Roman Empire

Hail Mary

Ave Maria
(AH vay) (mah REE ah)

Hail, Mary, full of grace,

Ave Maria, gratia plena,
(AH vay) (mah REE ah) (GRAHT see ah) (PLAY nah)

the Lord is with thee.

Dominus tecum.
(DOH mee noos) (TAY kum)

Blessed art thou among women,

Benedicta tu in mulieribus,
(bay nay DIHK tah) (too) (ihn) (moo lee AIR ee bus)

and blessed is the fruit of thy womb,

et benedictus fructus ventris tui,
(et) (bay nay DIHK tus) (FRUK toos) (VEN trihs) (TOO ee)

Jesus.

Iesus.
(YAY zoos)

Holy Mary, Mother of God,

Sancta Maria, Mater Dei,
(SAHNK tah) (mah REE ah) (MAH tair) (DAY ee)

pray for us sinners,

ora pro nobis peccatoribus,
(OH rah) (proh) (NOH bees) (pek a TOR ee bus)

now and at the hour of our death.

nunc, et in hora mortis nostrae.
(noonk) (et) (ihn) (HOR ah) (MOR tees) (NOHS tray)

Amen.

Amen.
(AH men)

The Lord's Prayer

Oratio   Dominica
(oh RAHT see oh) (doh MEE nee kah)

Our Father, who art in heaven,	Pater noster, qui es in caelis, *(PAH tair) (NOHS tair) (kwee) (es) (ihn) (CHAY lees)*
hallowed be thy name;	sanctificetur nomen tuum. *(sahnk tee fee CHAY tor) (NOH men) (TOO um)*
thy kingdom come;	Adveniat regnum tuum. *(ahd VAY nee aht) (REG num) (TOO um)*
thy will be done	Fiat voluntas tua, *(FEE aht) (voh LUN tahs) (TOO ah)*
on earth as it is in heaven.	sicut in caelo et in terra. *(SEE koot) (ihn) (CHAY loh) (et) (ihn) (TAIR ah)*
Give us this day our daily bread;	Panem nostrum quotidianum *(PAH nem) (NOH strum) (kwoh tee dee AH num)*
	da nobis hodie, *(dah) (NOH bees) (HOH dee ay)*
and forgive us our trespasses	et dimitte nobis debita nostra *(et) (dih MIHT tay) (NOH bees) (DAY bee tah) (NOH strah)*
as we forgive those	sicut et nos dimittimus *(SEE koot) (et) (nohs) (dee MEE tee mus)*
who trespass against us;	debitoribus nostris. *(day bee TOR ee bus) (NOH strees)*
and lead us not into temptation,	Et ne nos inducas in tentationem, *(et) (nay) (nohs) (ihn DOO kahs) (ihn) (ten taht see OH nem)*
but deliver us from evil.	sed libera nos a malo. *(sed) (LEE bair ah) (nohs) (ah) (MAH loh)*
Amen.	Amen. *(AH men)*

Prayer to the Holy Spirit

Come, Holy Spirit, fill the hearts of your faithful,
and kindle in them the fire of your love.
Send forth your Spirit and they shall be created,
and you will renew the face of the earth.

Hail Holy Queen

Hail, Holy Queen, Mother of Mercy,
our life, our sweetness, and our hope!
To you we cry,
poor banished children of Eve;
to you we send up our sighs,
mourning and weeping in this vale of tears.
Turn, then, most gracious advocate,
your eyes of mercy toward us;
and after this, our exile,
show to us the blessed fruit of your womb,
    Jesus.
O clement, O loving, O sweet Virgin Mary!

The Apostles' Creed

I believe in God,
the Father almighty,
Creator of heaven and earth,
and in Jesus Christ, his only Son,
    our Lord,
who was conceived by the Holy Spirit,
born of the Virgin Mary,
suffered under Pontius Pilate,
was crucified, died, and was buried;
he descended into hell;
on the third day he rose again from the
    dead;
he ascended into heaven,
and is seated at the right hand of God
    the Father almighty;
from there he will come to judge the
    living and the dead.
I believe in the Holy Spirit,
the holy catholic Church,
the communion of saints,
the forgiveness of sins,
the resurrection of the body,
and life everlasting.
Amen.

The Nicene Creed

I believe in one God,
the Father almighty,
maker of heaven and earth,
of all things visible and invisible.

I believe in one Lord, Jesus Christ,
the Only Begotten Son of God,
born of the Father before all ages,
God from God, Light from Light,
true God from true God,
begotten, not made, consubstantial with
   the Father;
through him all things were made.
For us men and for our salvation,
he came down from heaven,
and by the Holy Spirit was incarnate of
   the Virgin Mary,
and became man.

For our sake he was crucified under
   Pontius Pilate,
he suffered death and was buried,
and rose again on the third day
in accordance with the Scriptures.
He ascended into heaven
and is seated at the right hand of the
   Father.
He will come again in glory
to judge the living and the dead
and his kingdom will have no end.

I believe in the Holy Spirit, the Lord, the
   giver of life,
who proceeds from the Father and the
   Son,
who with the Father and the Son is
   adored and glorified,
who has spoken through the prophets.
I believe in one, holy, catholic and
   apostolic Church.
I confess one Baptism for the forgiveness
   of sins
and I look forward to the resurrection of
   the dead
and the life of the world to come. Amen.

Prayer Before the Blessed Sacrament

Lord Jesus, I believe that you are truly
present in the Eucharist.
As I receive you in
   Holy Communion,
help me to love as you loved,
serve as you served,
so I can be the Body
   of Christ to others.
Amen.

Grace After Meals

Father of mercy,
we praise you and give you glory
for the wonderful gifts you have given
us: for life and health, for faith and
love, and for this meal we have shared
    together.
Father, we thank you through Christ
our Lord. Amen.

Grace Before Meals

Bless us, O Lord, and these thy
gifts which we are about to
receive from thy bounty through
Christ our Lord. Amen.

Act of Faith

O my God, I firmly believe that you
are one God in three Divine Persons,
Father, Son, and Holy Spirit. I believe
that your divine Son became man
and died for our sins and that he
will come to judge the living and
the dead. I believe these and all
the truths which the Holy Catholic
Church teaches, because you have
revealed them who are eternal truth
and wisdom, who can neither deceive
nor be deceived. In this faith I intend
to live and die. Amen.

Memorare

Remember, O most gracious Virgin
Mary, that never was it known that
anyone who fled to thy protection,
implored thy help, or sought thy
intercession, was left unaided.
Inspired by this confidence I fly
unto thee, O Virgin of virgins, my
Mother. To thee do I come, before
thee I stand, sinful and sorrowful.
O Mother of the Word Incarnate,
despise not my petitions, but
in thy mercy hear and
answer me. Amen.

Act of Hope

O Lord God, I hope by your grace for the pardon of all my sins and after life here to gain eternal happiness because you have promised it who are infinitely powerful, faithful, kind, and merciful. In this hope I intend to live and die. Amen.

Act of Love

O Lord God, I love you above all things and I love my neighbor for your sake because you are the highest, infinite and perfect good, worthy of all my love. In this love I intend to live and die. Amen.

Act of Contrition

My God,
I am sorry for my sins
      with all my heart.
In choosing to do wrong
and failing to do good,
I have sinned against you
whom I should love above all things.
I firmly intend, with your help,
to do penance,
to sin no more,
and to avoid whatever leads me to sin.
Our Savior Jesus Christ
suffered and died for us.
In his name, my God, have mercy.
— *Rite of Penance*

Prayer to the Guardian Angel
(contemporary)

Angel sent by God to guide me,
be my light and walk beside me;
be my guardian and protect me;
on the paths of life direct me.

Prayer to the Guardian Angel
(traditional)

Angel of God, my Guardian dear,
to whom his love commits me here,
ever this day (or night) be at my side,
to light and guard, to rule and guide. Amen.

The Angelus

V. The angel of the Lord declared unto Mary.

R. And she conceived of the Holy Spirit.

Hail Mary,...

V. Behold the handmaid of the Lord

R. Let it be done unto me according to thy word.

Hail Mary,...

V. And the Word was made flesh

R. And dwelt among us.

Hail Mary,...

V. Pray for us, O holy Mother of God

R. That we may be made worthy of the promises of Christ

Let us pray: Pour forth, we beseech Thee, O Lord, Thy grace into our hearts, That we, to whom the Incarnation of Christ thy Son was made known by the message of an angel, may, by his Passion and Cross, be brought to the glory of his Resurrection through the same Christ, our Lord. Amen.

The Rosary

The Rosary is a special devotion dedicated to the Virgin Mary. Praying the Rosary helps us think about Jesus' life and his suffering, death, Resurrection, and Ascension. The main part of praying the Rosary is repeating the Lord's Prayer, a group of ten Hail Marys, and the Glory Be.

We pray the Rosary using rosary beads. The rosary beads help us keep track of our prayers. Each group of beads is called a decade. Before starting each decade, we think about an event from Jesus' or Mary's life. We call these events mysteries.

The mysteries of the Rosary are divided into four groups. These groups are called the Joyful Mysteries, the Sorrowful Mysteries, the Glorious Mysteries, and the Luminous Mysteries. Each group has five mysteries. We pray each of these groups on specific days of the week. The chart below names all the mysteries and tells on which days to pray them.

The diagram on the next page explains how to pray the Rosary. It shows which prayer to say on each bead. Use this diagram to help you pray the Rosary on your own, in class, or with your family.

The Mysteries of the Rosary

Joyful Mysteries
(Monday and Saturday)
1. The Annunciation
2. The Visitation
3. The Birth of Jesus
4. The Presentation of Jesus in the Temple
5. The Finding of Jesus in the Temple

Glorious Mysteries
(Wednesday and Sunday)
1. The Resurrection
2. The Ascension
3. The Coming of the Holy Spirit on the Apostles
4. The Assumption of Mary into Heaven
5. The Crowning of Mary as Queen of Heaven

Sorrowful Mysteries
(Tuesday and Friday)
1. The Agony in the Garden
2. The Scourging at the Pillar
3. The Crowing with Thorns
4. The Carrying of the Cross
5. The Crucifixion

The Luminous Mysteries
(Thursday)
1. The Baptism of Jesus
2. The Miracle at Cana
3. Jesus Proclaims the Kingdom of God
4. The Transfiguration of Jesus
5. The Institution of the Eucharist

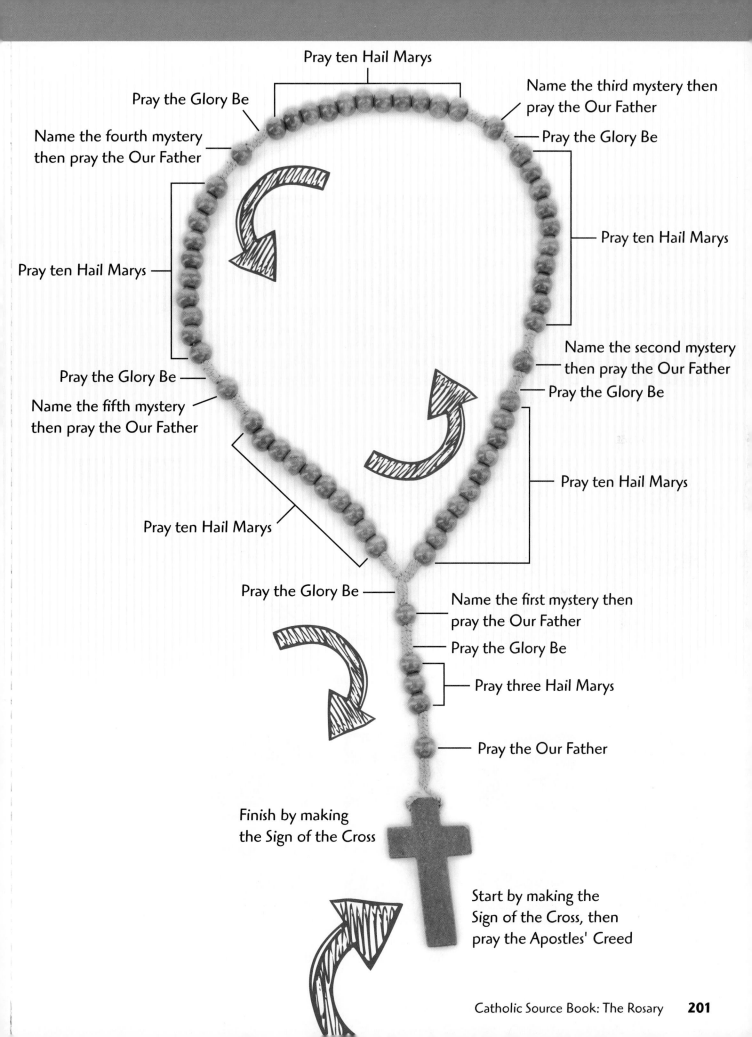

Pray ten Hail Marys

Pray the Glory Be

Name the third mystery then pray the Our Father

Name the fourth mystery then pray the Our Father

Pray the Glory Be

Pray ten Hail Marys

Pray ten Hail Marys

Pray the Glory Be

Name the fifth mystery then pray the Our Father

Name the second mystery then pray the Our Father

Pray the Glory Be

Pray ten Hail Marys

Pray ten Hail Marys

Pray the Glory Be

Name the first mystery then pray the Our Father

Pray the Glory Be

Pray three Hail Marys

Pray the Our Father

Finish by making the Sign of the Cross

Start by making the Sign of the Cross, then pray the Apostles' Creed

The Stations of the Cross

The Stations of the Cross are a special prayer devoted to Jesus. They help us think about the events of Jesus' suffering and death on the Cross. The Stations are usually prayed on the Fridays of Lent, but we can pray them any time.

1 Jesus is condemned to death

2 Jesus accepts the Cross

3 Jesus falls the first time

4 Jesus meets his mother

5 Simon helps Jesus carry the Cross

6 Veronica wipes the face of Jesus

7 Jesus falls the second time

8 Jesus meet the women of Jerusalem

9 Jesus falls the third time

10 Jesus is stripped of his garments

11 Jesus is nailed to the Cross

12 Jesus dies on the Cross

13 Jesus is taken down from the Cross

14 Jesus is buried in the tomb

Catholic Beliefs and Practices

The Ten Commandments

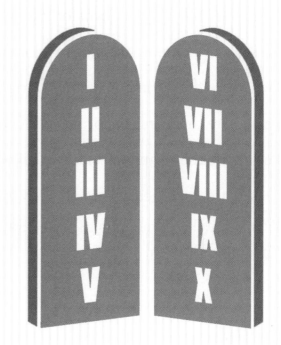

1. I am the LORD your God. You shall not have other gods besides me.

2. You shall not take the name of the LORD, your God, in vain.

3. Remember to keep holy the Sabbath day.

4. Honor your father and mother.

5. You shall not kill.

6. You shall not commit adultery.

7. You shall not steal.

8. You shall not bear false witness against your neighbor.

9. You shall not covet your neighbor's wife.

10. You shall not covet anything that belongs to your neighbor.

The Great Commandment

(The Two Commandments of Love)

- You shall love the Lord your God with all your heart, with all your soul, with all your mind, and with all your strength.

- You shall love your neighbor as yourself.
  (Matthew 22:37, Mark 12:28–31, Luke 10:27)

The New Commandment

- Love one another as I love you.
  (John 15:12)

The Beatitudes

Jesus taught us the Beatitudes during the Sermon on the Mount. They tell us how to live as part of the Kingdom of God.

Blessed are the poor in spirit, for theirs is the kingdom of heaven.

Blessed are they who mourn, for they will be comforted.

Blessed are the meek, for they will inherit the land.

Blessed are they who hunger and thirst for righteousness, for they will be satisfied.

Blessed are the merciful, for they will be shown mercy.

Blessed are the clean of heart, for they will see God.

Blessed are the peacemakers, for they will be called children of God.

Blessed are they who are persecuted for the sake of righteousness, for theirs is the kingdom of heaven.

—Matthew 5:1–10

The Precepts of the Church

1. You must attend Mass on Sundays and on the other Holy Days of Obligation.

2. Confess your sins at least once a year.

3. Receive Holy Communion at least once a year, during the Easter season.

4. Observe the Church's days of fasting and abstinence.

5. Help support the needs of the Church.

Days of Fast

(for those between 18 and 59 years of age)

Ash Wednesday, Good Friday

- To fast means to eat only one full meal and one or two small meals a day.

- We also fast for one hour before Communion. This means we have no food or drink, except water, in that time.

Days of Abstinence

(for those age 14 and older)

Ash Wednesday, All Fridays in Lent

- Abstinence means going without something. During Lent we abstain from eating meat on Ash Wednesday and all the Fridays of Lent.

Catholic Social Teaching

Jesus taught that we should treat one another with love and compassion. The Church helps us do so with teachings on social justice, called Catholic social teaching. Catholic social teaching helps create a world where we work together for the common good, as God wants.

Life and Dignity of the Human Person Every person is created in God's image, and every human life is sacred. We are called to treat all people with dignity, and to protect the rights of all people. This means we should also work to correct any injustices in our society.

Call to Family, Community, and Participation In order for our society to be healthy, we all have to contribute to it in good ways. We can start by showing care for our family and all families.

Solidarity All people are members of God's family. Like members of a family, we are all responsible for one another. Solidarity means we share with one another both spiritual goods and material goods.

Option for the Poor and Vulnerable God loves all people, and he calls us to love one another as he loves us. This especially means that we should care for those who are poor and help them have what they need to live.

Rights and Responsibilities Every person has a right to life and the right to live with dignity. This means every person has basic rights, and that we should work to protect those rights.

Care for God's Creation God is the Creator of all people and everything that exists in nature. He wants us to enjoy and care for his creation, for our generation and generations to come.

Option for the Poor and Vulnerable In society, there are people who are rich and people who are poor. We are called to protect and support those who are poor, so they can live with dignity.

The Works of Mercy

The Works of Mercy help us follow Jesus' teaching to love our neighbor. By putting the Works of Mercy into action, we can take care of others spiritually and physically. The Works of Mercy that care for people's physical needs are called the Corporal Works of Mercy. Those that care for spiritual needs are called the Spiritual Works of Mercy.

The Corporal Works of Mercy	The Spiritual Works of Mercy
Feed the hungry.	Counsel the doubtful.
Give drink to the thirsty.	Instruct the ignorant.
Clothe the naked.	Admonish sinners.
Shelter the homeless.	Console the suffering.
Visit the sick.	Forgive those who hurt you.
Visit the imprisoned.	Bear wrongs patiently.
Bury the dead.	Pray for the living and the dead.

The Gifts of the Holy Spirit

We receive these seven Gifts of the Holy Spirit in Confirmation.

- **Wisdom** is knowing and accepting God's will for us.
- **Understanding** is knowing how God wants us to live.
- **Counsel (Right Judgment)** is realizing the difference between what is morally good and what is sinful.
- **Fortitude (Courage)** is having the strength to do what is morally good, even when it is hard.
- **Knowledge** is discovering more about God.
- **Piety (Reverence)** is respecting and loving God.
- **Fear of the Lord (Wonder and Awe)** is recognizing God's greatness and always wanting to please him.

The Fruits of the Holy Spirit

The twelve Fruits of the Holy Spirit can also be called effects of the Holy Spirit. That is because the presence of the Holy Spirit strengthens these qualities in us.

- Charity
- Joy
- Peace
- Patience
- Kindness
- Goodness
- Generosity
- Gentleness
- Faithfulness
- Modesty
- Self-control
- Chastity

The Seven Capital (Deadly) Sins

The Seven Deadly Sins are sinful attitudes that hurt our relationship with God and others. They also can lead to more serious sin. We can overcome the deadly sins by practicing the virtues. (See the next two lists.)

- **Pride** is believing that we are better than others. Pride also means not recognizing the good qualities of others.
- **Greed** is wanting material things, such as money or possessions, very badly, even to the point of doing something wrong to get them.
- **Anger** is hatred toward another person and wanting to have revenge.
- **Envy** is jealousy of what someone else has, and being unhappy when something good happens for someone else because we want it for ourselves.
- **Gluttony** is eating far more than we need.
- **Sloth** is laziness, especially in the way we live our faith.
- **Lust** is like greed and envy. It is about wanting anything so much that it leads to sinful choices.

The Theological Virtues

These three virtues are habits that come from God and help us live in a relationship with the Blessed Trinity.

- **Faith** is believing in God and wanting to live in happiness with him.
- **Hope** is trusting God and relying on him.
- **Charity (Love)** is thinking about God and others with love, and showing that love through our good actions.

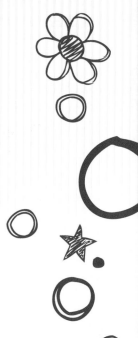

The Cardinal Virtues

These four virtues are also called the human virtues. We learn them as we learn about our faith. We strengthen them through practice.

- **Prudence** is being able to identify what is good and choosing to do it.
- **Justice** is caring about and respecting the needs of others, and working to be fair to others.
- **Fortitude** is the ability to resist temptation and choose what is good.
- **Temperance** is about having self-control. It means we are able to have balance between wants and needs in our lives.

Four Marks of the Church

The Marks of Church are four qualities that identify Christ's Church.

One	Holy
Catholic	Apostolic

The Seven Sacraments

The sacraments bring God's grace into our lives. They help us grow in holiness as members of the Church. There are three groups of sacraments.

Sacraments of Christian Initiation	Sacraments of Healing	Sacraments at the Service of Communion
Baptism Confirmation Eucharist These three sacraments celebrate our membership into the Church.	Penance and Reconciliation Anointing of the Sick In these two sacraments we receive God's grace for the healing of our mind, body, and spirit.	Matrimony Holy Orders These two sacraments celebrate people's commitment to serve God and others.

Holy Days of Obligation

We have an obligation to attend Mass on these holy days, and on every Sunday.

- **Solemnity of the Blessed Virgin Mary, the Mother of God,** January 1
- **Ascension of the Lord**, forty days after Easter
- **Assumption of the Blessed Virgin Mary**, August 15
- **All Saints' Day**, November 1
- **Immaculate Conception of the Blessed Virgin Mary**, December 8
- **Christmas**, December 25

Order of the Mass

The Introductory Rites
Entrance Chant
Greeting
Penitential Act
Kyrie (Lord, Have Mercy)
Gloria
Collect (Opening Prayer)

The Liturgy of the Word
First Reading
Responsorial Psalm
Second Reading
Gospel Acclamation
Gospel Reading
Homily
Profession of Faith
Prayer of the Faithful

The Liturgy of the Eucharist
Offertory Chant
Presentation and Preparation of the Gifts
Prayer over the Offerings
The Eucharistic Prayer
Sanctus (Holy, Holy, Holy)

The Communion Rite
The Lord's Prayer
Sign of Peace
Agnus Dei (Lamb of God)
Communion
Communion Song
Period of Silence or Song of Praise
Prayer after Communion

The Concluding Rites
Priest's Greeting and Blessing
Dismissal

Celebrating the Sacrament of Penance

Examination of Conscience

In an examination of conscience, you reflect on how well you have followed God's will. You prayerfully ask yourself if your words or actions have hurt your relationship with God or with other people. The following list of the Ten Commandments and questions will help you in your examination of conscience.

1 **I am the LORD your God, you shall not have other gods before me.** Do I always show my love for God? Do I always try to please him?

2 **You shall not take the name of the LORD, your God, in vain.** Do I always speak about God, Mary, and the saints with respect?

3 **Remember to keep holy the Sabbath.** Do I go to Mass every Sunday and on Holy Days of Obligation?

4 **Honor your father and mother.** Do I obey my parents and other adults who care for me? Do I listen to them with respect?

5 **You shall not kill.** Do I show respect for all human life? Do I treat others with kindness and love?

6 **You shall not commit adultery.** Do I treat my body and the bodies of others with respect?

7 **You shall not steal.** Have I taken anything that does not belong to me? Do I cheat or help others to cheat?

8 **You shall not bear false witness against your neighbor.** Do I always tell the truth, even when it is hard? Do I protect the reputations of others?

9 **You shall not covet your neighbor's wife.** Do I dress, talk, and act in a way that shows that I respect myself and others?

10 **You shall not covet your neighbor's goods.** Am I jealous of what others have? Do I wish that what others have belongs to me?

Steps for Celebrating the Sacrament of Penance

Remember that you can celebrate the Sacrament of Penance by speaking to the priest face to face or behind the screen.

1. **The priest welcomes you.** You tell him how long it has been since your last confession. You can use these words: "Bless me, Father, for I have sinned. It has been (number of weeks or months) since my last confession." The priest will lead you in making the Sign of the Cross.

2. **You listen to a Scripture reading.** The priest may read a short Scripture passage about God's love and mercy. Listen to the reading prayerfully.

3. **You confess your sins.** Think about the examination of conscience you completed. Tell the priest all the things that you have said or done that may have offended God. Do your best to tell all the sins you have committed. The priest will help you think about how you can avoid sin and please God. He will then give you a penance to complete. This may be a prayer and an act of kindness that you can do.

4. **You ask God for forgiveness.** You express sorrow for your sins and your love for God by praying an Act of Contrition.

5. **You receive absolution.** The priest extends his hands over your head. He says the prayer of absolution. He forgives your sins in the name of the Father, the Son, and the Holy Spirit.

6. **You say a prayer of thanksgiving.** The priest continues with these words: "Give thanks to the Lord, for he is good." You respond: "His mercy endures forever." After you leave the confessional, you take time to pray. If the priest asked you to pray a prayer for your penance, you pray it now. You thank God for his forgiveness. You promise God and yourself that you will try to please him.

The Liturgical Year

Your family probably celebrates many important occasions every year, such as birthdays and anniversaries. Your family also probably commemorates important events that happen during the year. These might include graduations or reunions, or sad events like the death of a family member or friend.

In the same way, the Church celebrates and remembers many important events each year. These events and the time to commemorate them are called the Church's feasts and seasons. The Church's calendar of feasts and seasons is called the **Liturgical Year**.

The Liturgical Year begins at Advent, when we are awaiting Jesus' birth. It continues with his birth, Passion, death, Resurrection, and Ascension, and our expectation of his return. Within the seasons of the Liturgical Year are also many feasts that mark special events in the life of Jesus, Mary, and the saints. A number of these days are Holy Days of Obligation. This means these days are so important we are required to attend Mass.

Here is a list of the seasons of the Liturgical Year. The diagram on page 213 shows when these seasons happen during the year.

Seasons of the Liturgical Year

Advent

During Advent we wait and prepare for Christ's birth. We also prepare for his return at the end of time. Advent begins four Sundays before Christmas and ends at the Christmas Eve Vigil Mass.

Traditional liturgical color: Purple
What the color means: Waiting

The Christmas Season

During the Christmas season we celebrate Jesus' birth and the events associated with it. The season begins at the Christmas Eve Vigil Mass. It ends on the Feast of the Baptism of the Lord.

Traditional liturgical colors: White and gold
What the colors means: Joy

Lent

During Lent we prepare for Jesus' Resurrection. We remember Jesus' Passion—his suffering and death on the Cross. We share in Jesus' suffering by making sacrifices and doing acts of charity, and especially through the liturgy and prayer. Lent begins on Ash Wednesday and ends on Holy Thursday evening.

Traditional liturgical color: Purple
What the color means: Penance

Easter Triduum

The Easter Triduum (tri-do-UM) begins with the Holy Thursday liturgy. It includes Good Friday, and ends on Easter Sunday evening. During these three days we recall the Last Supper, when Jesus instituted the Eucharist, Jesus' suffering and death, and his Resurrection.

Traditional liturgical colors: Red (on Good Friday) and white (the other days of the Triduum)
What the colors mean: Red is for Jesus' suffering; white is for joy

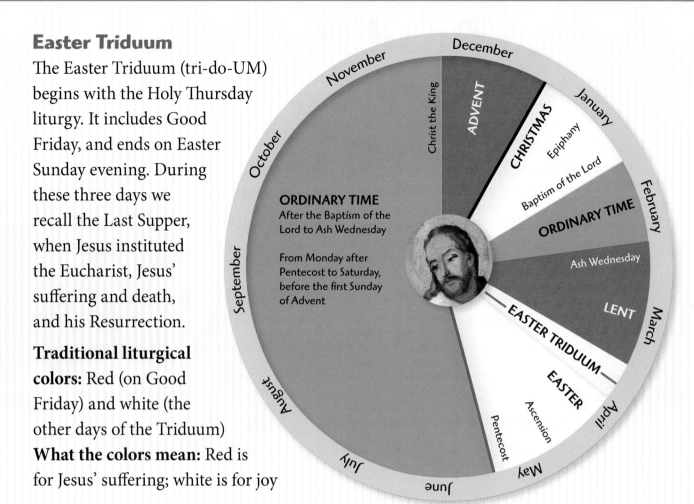

ORDINARY TIME
After the Baptism of the Lord to Ash Wednesday

From Monday after Pentecost to Saturday, before the first Sunday of Advent

The Easter Season

The Easter Season lasts for fifty days. It begins on Easter Sunday evening and lasts until Pentecost Sunday. During the Easter season we rejoice in Jesus' Resurrection and our salvation. We also celebrate Jesus' Ascension into Heaven.

Traditional liturgical color: White and gold (all the days of the season except Pentecost) and red (on Pentecost)
What the colors mean: White is for joy; red represents the coming of the Holy Spirit.

Ordinary Time

Ordinary Time takes place twice during the Liturgical Year: in the time between the end of the Christmas season and the start of Lent and between the end of the Easter season and the start of Advent. During Ordinary Time we celebrate and reflect on the events of Jesus' life and his teachings.

Traditional liturgical color: Green
What the color means: Hope

How to Read the Bible

Did you know that the Bible is a collection of many books? In fact, the Bible includes seventy-three books. These seventy-three books contain many different types of writing, such as poetry, or instructions and sayings, or history. Of all the books in the Bible, the Gospels have a very special place, because they tell us about the life of Jesus.

All the books of the Bible are organized into two main parts: the Old Testament and the New Testament. The Old Testament has 46 books and the New Testament has 27 books.

All the books of the Old Testament are from the time before Jesus. They tell about God's saving work before he sent Jesus to us. The books of the New Testament are about the life of Jesus and about the early Church. They teach us about Jesus' life and teachings, and that he is the Savior. They also tell us how Jesus' followers shared the Good News of Jesus and helped the Church grow.

Even though the books of the Bible were written by people, God is the author of everything in the Bible. That is why we call the Bible the Word of God.

Here are the books of the Bible.

The Old Testament

The Pentateuch		Historical Books		Wisdom Books		Prophetic Books	
Gn	Genesis	Jos	Joshua	Jb	Job	Is	Isaiah
Ex	Exodus	Jgs	Judges	Ps	Psalms	Jer	Jeremiah
Lv	Leviticus	Ru	Ruth	Prv	Proverbs	Lam	Lamentations
Nm	Numbers	1 Sm	1 Samuel	Eccl	Ecclesiastes	Bar	Baruch
Dt	Deuteronomy	2 Sm	2 Samuel	Sg	Song of Songs	Ez	Ezekiel
		1 Kgs	1 Kings	Wis	Wisdom	Dn	Daniel
		2 Kgs	2 Kings	Sir	Sirach	Hos	Hosea
		1 Chr	1 Chronicles			Jl	Joel
		2 Chr	2 Chronicles			Am	Amos
		Ezr	Ezra			Ob	Obadiah
		Neh	Nehemiah			Jon	Jonah
		Tb	Tobit			Mi	Micah
		Jdt	Judith			Na	Nahum
		Est	Esther			Hb	Habakkuk
		1 Mc	1 Maccabees			Zep	Zephaniah
		2 Mc	2 Maccabees			Hg	Haggai
						Zec	Zechariah
						Mal	Malachi

The New Testament

The Gospels and Acts

Mt	Matthew
Mk	Mark
Lk	Luke
Jn	John
Acts	Acts of the Apostles

The Pauline Letters (The Epistles)

Rom	Romans
1 Cor	1 Corinthians
2 Cor	2 Corinthians
Gal	Galatians
Eph	Ephesians
Phil	Philippians
Col	Colossians
1 Thes	1 Thessalonians
2 Thes	2 Thessalonians
1 Tm	1 Timothy
2 Tm	2 Timothy
Ti	Titus
Phlm	Philemon
Heb	Hebrews

The Catholic Letters and Revelation

Jas	James
1 Pt	1 Peter
2 Pt	2 Peter
1 Jn	1 John
2 Jn	2 John
3 Jn	3 John
Jude	Jude
Rv	Revelation

How to Find a Scripture Passage

Each book of the Bible, such as the Book of Exodus or the Gospel of Luke, is divided into chapters. Each chapter is divided into verses. To find a story or passage in the Bible, we use the name of the book of the Bible, along with the chapter number and verse numbers. Here's an example:

Luke 10:29–37

Here are the steps for finding the passage in your Bible.

1. Find the Bible book you are looking for. You can use the table of contents to find the page number where the book begins.

2. Find the chapter in the book.

3. Find the first verse of the passage. To find the verse, use the small numbers in the text. The passage includes all the verses between the two numbers, including the last verse. (In this example, you would read verses 29 through 37.)

4. Start reading!

The name of the book → LUKE 10 ← **The chapter number**

1578

have observed Satan fall like lightning* from the sky.[p] [19]Behold, I have given you the power 'to tread upon serpents' and scorpions and upon the full force of the enemy and nothing will harm you.[q] [20]Nevertheless, do not rejoice because the spirits are subject to you, but rejoice because your names are written in heaven."[r]

Praise of the Father.[s] [21]At that very moment he rejoiced [in] the holy Spirit and said, "I give you praise, Father, Lord of heaven... you have hi... **The verse numbers** ... and the learned you have revealed them to the childlike.* Yes, Father, such has been your gracious will.[t] [22]All things have been handed over to me by my Father. No one knows who the Son is except the Father, and who the Father is except the Son and anyone to whom the Son wishes to reveal him."[u]

The Privileges of Discipleship.[v] [23]Turning to the disciples in private he said, "Blessed are the eyes that see what you see. [24]For I say to you, many prophets and kings desired to see what you see, but did not see it, and to hear what you hear, but did not hear it."

The Greatest Commandment.[w]

with all your strength, and with all your mind, and your neighbor as yourself. [28]He replied to him, "You have answered correctly; do this and you will live."[z]

The Parable of the Good Samaritan. [29]But because he wished to justify himself he said to Jesus, "And who is my neighbor?" [30]Jesus replied, "A man fell victim to robbers as he went down from Jerusalem to Jericho. They stripped and beat him and went off leaving him half-dead. [31]A priest happened to be going down that road, but when he saw him, he passed by on the opposite side. [32]Likewise a Levite came to the place, and when he saw him, he passed by on the opposite side. [33]But a Samaritan traveler who came upon him was moved with compassion at the sight. [34]He approached the victim, poured oil and wine over his wounds and bandaged them. Then he lifted him up on his own animal, took him to an inn and cared for him. [35]The next day he took out two silver coins and gave them to the innkeeper with the instruction, 'Take care of him. If you spend more than what I have given you, I shall repay you on my way back.' [36]Which of these three, in your opinion, was neighbor to the robbers' victim?" [37]He answered, "The one who treated him with mercy." Jesus said to him, "Go and do likewise."

The *Catechism of the Catholic Church*

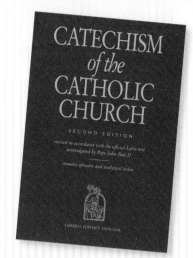

A catechism is a book that teaches about the faith. The *Catechism of the Catholic Church* teaches us about our Catholic faith. It explains the Church's teachings and what we believe as Catholics. It tells us about the Church's liturgy and the sacraments. It teaches about the Ten Commandments and how to follow them in our lives. It also teaches us about how to have a relationship with God through prayer.

The *Catechism of the Catholic Church* is organized into four main parts. Here are the four parts and some examples of what you can learn. The numbers in parentheses tell you the paragraph number where you can read more about each teaching in the *Catechism*.

I | The Profession of Faith; The Profession of the Christian Faith

- By listening to our conscience and through creation we can know that God exists. God is Creator and the cause and end of everything. (*CCC*, 46)
- Faith requires us to open our minds and hearts to God. (*CCC*, 176)
- Jesus Christ is God's Son made man. He is the image of the invisible God. (*CCC*, 381)
- Jesus' title "Son of God" helps us know the eternal relationship of Jesus Christ to God his Father. (*CCC*, 454)
- Jesus Christ is truly God and truly man. For this reason he is the one and only mediator between God and man. (*CCC*, 480)
- The Incarnation is the mystery of the union of the divine and human natures of Jesus Christ in one Person. (*CCC*, 483)
- Non-Catholics who believe in Jesus Christ and have been baptized are in a certain, but imperfect, communion with the Catholic Church. (*CCC*, 838)
- Through no fault of their own, some people do not know the Gospel. If they seek God with a sincere heart they may achieve eternal salvation. (*CCC*, 847)
- Jesus entrusted the Church with the mission to bring the Good News of salvation to all people in all time. (*CCC*, 849)
- Religious life is characterized by the public profession of the evangelical counsels of poverty, chastity, and obedience. (*CCC*, 944)

II The Celebration of the Christian Mystery; The Seven Sacraments of the Church

- An indulgence is the remission of the temporal punishment due to sins already forgiven by God. We can obtain indulgences for ourselves and also for the souls in Purgatory through good works or prayers. (*CCC*, 1498)
- Through Baptism we are born to new life in Christ. We are strengthened by Confirmation, and we are nourished by the Eucharist. (*CCC*, 1275)
- Jesus is truly present in the consecrated bread and wine. Because of this we call the Eucharist the Sacrament of the Real Presence of Jesus. (*CCC*, 1413)

III Life in Christ; Man's Vocation: Life in the Spirit

- The morality, or goodness, of our actions depends on the action itself and our intention. The circumstances can affect the goodness or sinfulness of an act. However, some actions are always sinful, no matter the circumstances. For example, hurting a person who cannot defend himself or herself is always wrong. (*CCC*, 1747, 1761)
- We can be worthy in God's sight because of his gift of grace and our response. (*CCC*, 2025)
- Atheism is denying the existence of God. It is a sin against the First Commandment. (*CCC*, 2140)
- Our veneration, or reverence, of sacred images has its basis in the Incarnation. Venerating sacred images does not violate the First Commandment. (*CCC*, 2141)
- The Second Commandment forbids us from calling on God to be a witness to a lie. This is a sin called perjury, and it is a serious offense against God, who is always faithful to his promises. (*CCC*, 2163)
- Sins against the truth violate the Eighth Commandment. We must always be truthful. (*CCC*, 2507, 2508)
- When we celebrate the Sacrament of Penance, the priest is forbidden from sharing what we tell him with anyone. This is called the sacramental seal. (*CCC*, 2511)

IV Christian Prayer; Prayer in the Christian Life

- The Church encourages devotional practices that help us proclaim our faith and strengthen our relationship with God. (*CCC*, 2708, 2720)
- The Lord's Prayer is the summary of the whole Gospel. (*CCC*, 2774)
- Through prayer, we are united with God the Father and with his Son, Jesus Christ. (*CCC*, 2799)

Glossary

Annunciation the angel Gabriel's announcement to Mary God had chosen her to be the Mother of Jesus (*page 55*)

Ascension when the Risen Jesus was taken up to Heaven to be with God the Father forever (*page 33*)

Assumption the teaching that after her earthly life, Mary was taken into Heaven, body and soul, to be with God (*page 57*)

Beatitudes Jesus' teachings about how to live as part of the Kingdom of God (*page 151*)

Blessed Sacrament a name for the Holy Eucharist, especially the Body of Christ kept in the Tabernacle (*page 77*)

Blessed Trinity one God in three Divine Persons—God the Father, God the Son, and God the Holy Spirit (*page 25*)

Body of Christ a name for the Church. Christ is the head of the Church, and all the baptized are members of the Body. (*page 49*)

Communion of Saints everyone who believes in and follows Jesus — people on earth and people who have died and are in Purgatory or Heaven (*page 129*)

conscience the God-given ability that helps us know right from wrong (*page 93*)

contemplation a way of praying by simply being in the presence of God and focusing on our love for him (*page 165*)

covenant a sacred promise or agreement between God and humans, such as the covenants he made with Noah and Abraham (*page 25*)

creation everything in the world made by God (*page 111*)

devotions forms of prayer that are separate from the Mass and the sacraments (*page 181*)

Divine Revelation the way God makes himself, and his plan for all people, known to us (*page 17*)

Doctor of the Church a title the Church gives to people whose writings have helped others understand the faith (*page 175*)

evangelization sharing the Good News of Jesus through words and actions in a way that invites people to accept the Gospel (*page 41*)

faith a gift from God that leads us to believe in him and obey him *(page 15)*

free will our God-given freedom and ability to make choices *(page 119)*

grace God's free and loving gift to us of his own life and help *(page 85)*

Heaven the full joy of living with God forever *(page 65)*

Hell being separated from God forever because of a choice to turn away from him and not ask for forgiveness *(page 65)*

Immaculate Conception the truth that God kept Mary free from sin from the first moment she came into being *(page 57)*

Incarnation the mystery that the Son of God became man to save all people *(page 33)*

Kingdom of God the world of love, peace, and justice that is in Heaven and is still being built on earth *(page 63)*

Last Judgment God's final victory over evil that will happen at the end of time. At that time, Christ will return and judge all the living and the dead. *(page 63)*

Last Supper the meal Jesus shared with his disciples on the night before he died. At the Last Supper, Jesus gave himself in the Eucharist. *(page 75)*

lay people all of the baptized people in the Church who share in God's mission but are not ordained; sometimes called the laity *(page 101)*

liturgy the official public worship of the Church. The Eucharist is the Church's most important liturgy. *(page 77)*

Magisterium the teaching office of the Church, which is all of the bishops in union with the Pope *(page 17)*

Mass the Church's prayer of praise and thanksgiving to God; the celebration of the Eucharist *(page 77)*

meditation thinking about God and his presence in our lives *(page 165)*

mercy kindness and concern for those who are suffering. God has mercy on us even though we are sinners. *(page 91)*

ministry a way of being a sign of the Kingdom of God by caring for and serving others *(page 99)*

miracle an amazing or wonderful event that happens by the power of God *(page 99)*

missionary a person who answers God's call to help people all over the world know about Jesus *(page 131)*

moral in right relationship with God, yourself, and others *(page 129)*

mortal sin a serious sin that separates us from God and his grace *(page 93)*

natural law rules about goodness that are written in our hearts and are natural to follow *(page 137)*

novena a series of prayers for a specific intention prayed over nine days *(page 181)*

Original Sin the sin of our first parents, Adam and Eve, which led to the sinful condition of all people *(page 85)*

papal infallibility the gift of the Holy Spirit given to the Pope and the bishops in union with him to teach about faith and morals without error *(page 49)*

parable a short story Jesus told about everyday life to teach something about God *(page 63)*

Paschal Mystery the suffering, death, Resurrection, and Ascension of Jesus Christ *(page 33)*

Pentecost the feast that celebrates the coming of the Holy Spirit fifty days after Easter *(page 39)*

prophet a person God has chosen to speak in his name *(page 31)*

Purgatory a state of final purification after death and before entering into Heaven *(page 65)*

Resurrection Jesus being raised from the dead three days after his death on the Cross *(page 33)*

sacrament a special sign and celebration that Jesus gave his Church. The sacraments allow us to share in the life and work of God. *(page 75)*

Sacrament of Eucharist the sacrament in which, through the ministry of the priest and by the power of the Holy Spirit, Jesus shares himself, and the bread and wine become his Body and Blood *(page 75)*

Sacraments at the Service of Communion the two sacraments that celebrate people's commitment to serve God and the community: Holy Orders and Matrimony *(page 101)*

Sacraments of Christian Initiation the three sacraments that celebrate membership into the Church: Baptism, Confirmation, and Eucharist *(page 85)*

Sacraments of Healing Penance and the Anointing of the Sick. In these sacraments, God heals our mind, body, and spirit. *(page 93)*

Sacred Scripture another name for the Bible; Sacred Scripture is the Word of God written by humans *(page 17)*

Sacred Tradition God's Word handed down to all the faithful in the Church's creed, sacraments and other teachings *(page 17)*

sin a deliberate thought, word, deed, or omission that goes against God's law. Sins hurt our relationship with God and other people. *(page 91)*

soul the spiritual part of a human that lives forever *(page 65)*

stewardship caring for and protecting the gifts of creation that God has given us *(page 113)*

Tabernacle the special place in church where the Blessed Sacrament is reserved after Mass *(page 77)*

temptation wanting to do something we should not or not doing something we should *(page 119)*

Ten Commandments the laws that God gave Moses on Mount Sinai. They tell us what is required to love God and others *(page 137)*

venial sin a less serious sin against God's law that weakens our relationship with him *(page 93)*

virtues good spiritual habits that make us stronger and help us do what is right and good *(page 121)*

Works of Mercy loving acts of caring for the physical and spiritual needs of other people *(page 153)*

Index